"TO ENCOURAGE THE ART OF THE FILM"

"To encourage the art of the film"

The story of the
British Film Institute

IVAN BUTLER

Foreword by
RICHARD ATTENBOROUGH

ROBERT HALE · LONDON

© *Ivan Butler 1971*
First published in Great Britain 1971

ISBN 0 7091 2409 0

Robert Hale & Company
63 Old Brompton Road
London S.W.7

PRINTED AND BOUND IN GREAT BRITAIN BY C. TINLING & CO. LTD.
LONDON AND PRESCOT

Contents

Illustrations

The title of this book is taken from the
Articles of Association of the British Film
Institute, paragraph 3 (September 1933).

Foreword

It is, perhaps, inevitable that so many of those involved or interested in the numerous and varied aspects of motion pictures should tend, at best, to take The British Film Institute for granted and, at worst, to use it as an all-too-convenient Aunt Sally for the expression of such criticism as any similar organisation is bound to face. One salient fact, however, is surely indisputable—the Institute embraces a field of activities and responsibilities so wide that their non-existence would be utterly unthinkable. Nevertheless, they are palpably not available from any other source.

It is certainly not my intention to enumerate here the purposes, development and performance of The British Film Institute. These have been comprehensively and lucidly recorded by Mr. Butler. However, to take just one example among its many operations, think for a moment of the calamitous void in the fabric of the British Film structure that would be brought about by the total absence of the National Film Archive.

To represent this book as a full record of and a comprehensive reference to the history and work of the Institute would be an accurate, though incomplete, description—for Mr. Butler has been, from the beginning, determined that his readers should also be entertained. In the achievement of this aim, he has met with complete success. For this is no sycophantic account commissioned by the Institute itself. The idea for such a book was Mr. Butler's own and he has described the Institute in all its ramifications as he found it, without fear or favour. His admirable study will surely be of tremendous interest, not only to all those in any way concerned with the Film Industry itself, but also to a vast number of readers not actively involved with the cinema.

R.A.

Preface

The British Film Institute has been described by one of its Directors as "perhaps the most complex and highly developed organisation of its kind in Europe, and probably the world".* In such cases a chronicler is always faced with the problem of how best and most clearly to present the story he has to tell. To have followed a completely chronological path would, it seemed to me, have resulted in an unwieldy mass of material with numerous and confusing digressions. I decided instead to concentrate in the first part of the book on an outline history of the Institute's development as an organisation up to late 1970, mentioning only briefly its varying activities as they came into being or had some special significance. These activities are then dealt with separately, and a final section briefly looks toward the future.

This method, besides making for clarity, will, I hope, prove convenient for anybody who may be particularly interested in one section of the Institute's work (e.g. the National Film Theatre, the Archive, or the Film Production Board), and who will thus be able to follow its development straight through without having to jump from page to page with the help of the index. All these varying concerns are, obviously, interlocking branches of one tree, and it is only for the sake of convenience that they are treated as separate departments. I have also endeavoured not to overload the narrative with arrays of figures, entering membership numbers and financial details, for example, as occasional signposts rather than complete records.

In referring to foreign films I have used the title most frequently found in Britain, e.g. *The Seventh Seal, Porte des Lilas, Hand in the Trap, L'Avventura.*

The general history of the BFI falls rather neatly into sections according to the period of office of each Director – though these

---

* *The Film and Television as an Aspect of European Culture*, by James Quinn, pub. A. W. Sijthoff – Leyden, 1968.

are, of course arbitrary divisions, the progress of the BFI being one of continuing development, and the work of its Directors always involving the closest association with their fellow officers, Chairmen, and Board of Governors. With Denis Forman, James Quinn and Stanley Reed I have had lengthy sessions. Oliver Bell, who did so much for the Institute in the difficult years before, during, and just after the Second World War is, unhappily, no longer living, but I was fortunately able to call upon Olwen Vaughan, who was Secretary during most of his years in office. In the various departments I have also received much help from Ernest Lindgren, Sir Michael Balcon, Leslie Hardcastle, John Huntley, Paddy Whannel, Philip Strick, Brenda Davies, Gillian Hartnoll and the staff of the Information Department, Molly Lloyd, Bruce Beresford, Ken Wlaschin, Bobby Brown, Enid Law, Vernon Saunders, Penelope Houston, Barrie Wood, Clyde Jeavons, Roger Holman, Colin Ford, Sheila Whitaker, Søren Fischer, Diane Jupp, Molly Kershaw, Jackie Powell, and Harold Brown who spent an afternoon taking me around the Archive Buildings at Aston Clinton and Kingshill. To all these, and to many others connected with the BFI who have given me such willing assistance, I gladly acknowledge my indebtedness. I should also like to thank especially Jane Mercer and the members of the Press Office; Brian Baxter not only for information about NFT 2 but because it was through his intermediary offices that the book originally got under way; and above all Stanley Reed, the present Director, for his help, encouragement, and readiness to place his time at my disposal throughout the writing of it.

At the same time I would emphasise that at no time and in no way has any censorship been imposed on anything I wished to write – save only possibly the occasional subconscious censorship of individual amnesia. The minutes of the governors' meetings and other papers have been open for my inspection. I think this needs to be stated because, like any organisation of this nature, and particularly if it is in part financed by public money, the BFI has been – and probably always will be – accused from time to time of hiding things from its members and from the public eye, of censoring reports, of suppressing uncomfortable facts in order to preserve an 'image'. Doubtless in its thirty-seven years certain matters may have been pushed under the carpet: I can only say that, as far as I was concerned, it was not tacked down.

This book is intended as the story of an organisation concerned with the film, not a study of the aesthetics of the cinema: it accepts as obvious truth the contention (still sometimes questioned) that the film at its best is as valid an art form as music, literature or painting, for unless this is so the BFI, as it is constituted today, has no reason to exist.

I.B.

I

Organisation

BEGINNINGS

The year 1929 saw the final triumph of the talking film over its silent predecessor. By the autumn, nearly five thousand theatres in the United States had been wired for sound: the last silent picture of any note, Greta Garbo's *The Kiss*, was released in the autumn. In Britain by the end of the year all the large houses, and the majority of small ones, had installed the costly but unavoidable equipment, and a major production, Alfred Hitchcock's *Blackmail*, in which sound had been used with great imagination and ingenuity, had been shown. In the same year, faced with the realisation of the power, for good or ill, which the new dimension would add to the film, the British Institute of Adult Education held a conference which resulted in the formation of a Commission on Education and Cultural Films.

Its report, "The Film in National Life", was published in May, 1932. The principal recommendation was the establishment of a Film Institute "to promote the various uses of the film as a contribution to national well-being". A Certificate of Incorporation under the Companies Act of 1929 was received from the Board of Trade on 30th September 1933, and the future Institute's objects were defined as the encouragement of "the use and development of the cinematograph as a means of entertainment and instruction." A number of ancillary objects were also set out, including the establishment and maintenance of a national repository of films of permanent value – which later evolved into one of the Institute's most important functions, the formation of the National Film Archive.

The central control was vested in a council of nine governors with a chairman.* Thus the constitution resembles that of the BBC in that it is independent of the Government, although its governors are appointed by a senior Minister. The nine were chosen to represent equally education (C. J. Cleland, A. C. Cameron, John Buchan), the trade (R. S. Lambert, J. J. Lawson, C. M. Woolf) and the general public (Thomas Ormiston, Lady Levita, F. W. Baker). The Chairman was the Duke of Sutherland. J. W. Brown, of the British Institute of Adult Education, was appointed General Manager, as the post of Director was then called, and Reginald V. Crow, one time President of the Cinematograph Exhibitors Association, was Secretary.

Safeguards were agreed upon to protect the Institute from any inclination to interfere with film censorship or intrude on matters of purely trade interest.

Finance was provided by a grant from the Cinematograph Fund, a levy payable by cinemas in England and Wales on Sunday admissions. For some years this was the only source of revenue apart from members' subscriptions, receipts from the sale of publications and from film hire, and a couple of small items from the Home Office and the Ministry of Education.

The first meeting of governors took place on 5th October 1933 at 21 Panton Street, SW1, and later the same month the Institute was lodged in its first home when premises were rented on the first floor of 4 Great Russell Street, WC1.

As Denis Forman states: "In form it was a non-profit making limited liability company – in function it was to fulfil a wide range of purposes."† The birth of the young organisation was not given an unqualified welcome: despite the strong educational bias of its early years there were fears among the industry that it might encroach on commercial pastures, and among the film societies that it might interfere with their own activities in the raising of public appreciation of film as an art form. Assurances were hastily given in both cases. It is, in fact, interesting to note that one of the first of many attacks on the BFI during its existence

* After the Radcliffe Report of 1948 this number was enlarged and made more flexible: it now varies between ten and twenty.

† Supplementary article in *The Film and the Public*, by Roger Manvell (Pelican Books, 1955)

came in 1934 in a booklet entitled "The British Film Institute Exposed", declaring that it was unworthy to receive grants from the Cinema Fund because, among other failings, it had fallen under the control of the film trade. The booklet, written by a Mr Walter Ashley, was later withdrawn. The film industry's chief fear at this time was that the BFI might start producing films itself, or set itself up as an unofficial arbiter on commercial productions. The reply was that it would not and could not produce its own films, and had no intention of exercising censorship in the restrictive sense since "the whole case for a Film Institute rests on the belief that constructive action to encourage good films is better than restrictive action to discourage bad ones." On whose judgment the division into 'good' and 'bad' rested was not stated, and it could be argued that this statement of intent itself opened the way to a form of censorship.

Once the new organisation was established things began to happen with commendable speed. An early step was the taking over of the publication *Sight and Sound*, originally founded by the British Institute of Adult Education, and the launching of the *Monthly Film Bulletin*, a review of current film releases which is now an indispensable work of reference. Lectures were inaugurated in 1934 by Clifford Collinson to propagate the aims of the Institute and to encourage membership. Local branches were established in the provinces, and a number of film societies already in existence became allied to the BFI. In the autumn of 1934 the Scottish Film Council was formed as an integral part of the Institute but with a larger degree of autonomy than was the case with other branches.

The question as to whether the BFI should itself show films to the public came under discussion, but, without the facilities for doing this its activities were, in these early years, inevitably confined in the main to advice, liaison work between trade and cultural or educational bodies, and attempts to promote interest in 'better' films. Even so, and despite the continuing emphasis on education (*Sight and Sound* in autumn 1934 inaugurated a special eight-page section on *Films and the School*), the young Institute rapidly acquired a wide range of varied responsibilities. Committees and panels were formed on subjects such as the use of film in connection with medicine, geography, physical education, the Dominions, India and the colonies, and scientific research (proposing to investigate the psychological effects on audiences of certain types of films). Bodies approaching the BFI for differing forms of help included the Ulster Society for the Prevention of Cruelty to Animals, the Western Electric Co., the National Union of Teachers, the Library Association, the Geologists' Association, the International Missionary Council. A concern known as the Clean Film Movement, run by Mr J. Payton, sought the Institute's support and wanted to use the *Monthly Film Bulletin* to further its views. The suggestion was tactfully turned down, and the dangers pointed out of the *Bulletin* becoming other than a confidential (as it then was) document for members. The Movement, if it still exists, must be finding its hands full in dealing with the contemporary film scene.

An association which lasted for several years was that with the Cinema Christian Council (later named the Christian Cinema and Religious Film Society), and sections on its activities appeared in both *Sight and Sound* and the *Monthly Film Bulletin*. Grants were made to the society until 1941, when it was considered by the Board that its policy had so far deviated from its original intentions that no further action should be taken.

A sub-committee was set up to explore the possibility of a children's film company, and suggestions were made for the establishment of a course of cinematography at the University of London. Neither of these proposals was adopted, though both ideas have been developed in different forms since. Practical and technical matters such as the dangers of celluloid film in toy projectors, the quality of sub-standard 16mm stock and a testing code for daylight projection also came before the Board. It is interesting to note that several years after the arrival of sound in the commercial cinema there was still a general consensus of opinion that silent film was more practical for classroom purposes. Recognition of the Institute's growing influence – still mainly in the field of education – is indicated by the fact that it was entrusted with the task (which it still carries out) of certifying films as educational for duty-free import; and by such individual instances as a request from British International Pictures that their special 1935 Jubilee film, *Royal Cavalcade*, should be viewed by the BFI for recommendation to educational establishments. A resolution expressing the desirability of historical accuracy in entertainment pictures seems, however, to have had regrettably little effect.

Finally, 1935 saw the launching of the National Film Library, later renamed the National Film Archive, destined to develop into one of the most consistently successful of all the Institute's projects.

2. *1936 to 1948*

With all this external activity went a certain lack of internal organisation. Olwen Vaughan, who joined the Institute in 1935 as Secretary, describes the conditions as, frankly, chaotic. "There wasn't even a petty cash account. When money was needed for minor expenses, the secretary took it out of his pocket!" Miss Vaughan, who was to be very active in the affairs of the BFI for the next ten years, joined the staff through her father, the Reverend Frank Heming Vaughan, who was the founder of the original Merseyside Film Society in Liverpool, and was keenly interested in the new organisation. A fanatical filmgoer herself, she noticed with surprise that "I was one of the very few people concerned with the Institute who ever saw a film, and nearly all the contacts with actual film-makers such as Jean Renoir and Robert Flaherty (both early visitors) were made by me."

A policy to increase the contact between the BFI and the artistic and production side of the cinema did not make much headway. The emphasis was still heavily on Film and School. It was probably owing to this fact that, despite the varying activities and considerable publicity, actual membership numbers were somewhat slow in growing. By November 1936 the total was 755: the thousand mark was reached one year later.

Premises were found for the Film Library in Denmark Street, Soho, and these also contained a small viewing theatre. The latter was anything but palatial. Olwen Vaughan, one of whose interests was the promotion of film shows to convicted prisoners, remembers inviting members of the Home Office to see a selected programme. Entering the auditorium just in front of them, she found five large defunct rats proudly laid out in a row for her inspection by a conscientious rodent officer. Shortly afterwards extra room was leased in Great Russell Street and the top floor, formerly a carpet store-room, was converted into a theatre seating about twenty people. Designed by Miss Vaughan together with Lotte Reiniger, the renowned German director famous for her exquisite silhouette films, this viewing theatre is still in use today.

In 1936 the internal stresses and strains culminated in a happening which, though containing elements of wild farce, in fact caused the Institute considerable embarrassment and, when details were published in the press, ridicule. This – sounding rather like one of the stranger adventures of Sherlock Holmes – was the Celebrated Affair of the Talking Mongoose. Even today references to the Affair are apt to cause deprecating smiles, and records are not to be found in the archives. One of the most important and highly valued members of the Governing Board was R. S. Lambert, a member also of the BBC, and founder and editor of *The Listener*. Lambert was a close friend of Harry Price, famous ghost-hunter, and founder of the National Laboratory of Psychical Research. Interested in the possible use of film for recording psychic phenomena, Price had connections with the BFI, and in fact, as will be seen in the section on the Archive, had been adopted as Chairman of the NFL. Stories, which he passed on to Lambert, had reached him from a remote part of the Isle of Man of a mongoose which was distinguishing itself by chatting with farmers, throwing things around, and in general behaving in an unconventional and unusual manner. Lambert, always curious about anything out of the ordinary, joined Price in an investigation. The results of their enquiry were published in a book entitled *The Haunting of Cashen's Gap*. The whole affair of the super-mongoose might have been dismissed as a rather good joke but the disapproval of a member of the Board led to a suggestion being made to Gladstone Murray of the BBC that a person who endeavoured to carry on conversations with a mongoose was not very well suited to a position of responsibility in so dignified a concern as the BFI. The results of this grave accusation led to an action for libel being brought by Lambert, who was awarded substantial damages. The ensuing publicity caused a good deal of unkind laughter at the Institute's expense, which might have had quite a disastrous effect on the respect so vital at this stage of its development. Fortunately, in a general shake-up which took place just after the affair the Governors selected, as General Manager, Oliver Bell. Apart from sitting on a few committees concerned mainly with religious films, Bell had little knowledge of the cinema. His main interest had been in the theatre, in which connection he was chairman of the Pilgrim Players. He was a J.P. on the Wimbledon Bench and was later to become secretary-general of the Magistrates' Association. Though his main concern was with visual education and children's films, Bell proved himself a most capable, tactful and efficient Director (the title was changed during his period of office), ably steering the Institute through the difficult times preceding and during the war.

In the same year Sir Charles Cleland succeeded the Duke of Sutherland as chairman, and was himself followed by Sir George Clark in 1938 and Sir William Brass (later Lord Chattisham) in 1939.

Throughout the mid-thirties the BFI continued to extend its connections with the film societies. Among the earliest to become affiliated were Maidstone and Bristol. Merseyside was accepted as a branch member in February 1934, Leeds and Brighton, Hove & District in July 1934, Manchester and Chichester in February 1935, Colwyn Bay and North Wales, and Cardiff and South Wales, in 1936, Bradford and York in 1937. Many societies later dropped the word 'Institute' from their titles, but retained their connection. In 1939 about ten grants ranging from £20 to £120 were made by the BFI to film societies. Other grants included £400 to the Scottish Film Council and £400 (the last to be given) to the Cinema Christian Council.

At the outbreak of the war the Institute's policy was defined: "to continue the increase in the use of films in teaching, to continue the National Film Library, stimulate film appreciation, maintain information, and in general to see that the British film industry was not allowed to languish and die as in the 1914–18 war." As is now history, the British film – though production numbers fell to some extent – reached standards during the war years which it had seldom if ever attained before, in such features as *In Which We Serve, Next of Kin, The First of the Few, The Young Mr Pitt, The Way to the Stars, Blithe Spirit,* Olivier's *Henry V, The Way Ahead,* and the poetic semi-documentaries of Humphrey Jennings. For the Institute itself, however, these were difficult and frustrating years. "Many people were doing war work," says Miss Vaughan, "and I was left to mind the babies." The premises at Great Russell Street were badly damaged by blast quite early in the blitz, and though there were no casualties many records were lost.

The *Monthly Film Bulletin* and *Sight and Sound* both continued throughout the war, but the latter in particular suffered from the inevitable restrictions. All the films in the Library (like those of the industry itself) had to be removed, by Government order, from central London where their high inflammability made them a source of danger. Transport to a temporary refuge in the country was arranged by the BFI's Assistant Director, Robin Dickinson, with the assistance of its Technical Director, Hubert Waley (brother of the famous Chinese scholar Arthur Waley), and the Archive's present Film Preservation Officer, Harold Brown, who loaded the films on to a van and travelled with them to a disused stable in Rudgwick in Sussex, as a temporary refuge.

After the fall of France a series of French films was shown by Olwen Vaughan on Sunday nights at the Royal Empire Society's premises in Northumberland Avenue for the Free French forces, much of the material being obtained from the Institute Library. She also founded the French Club in St James's Place, SW1, which has become the temporary home and meeting place for visiting film directors from all over the world, and is still active after nearly thirty years.

In the six years of war current membership increased by just over 600, from 1,021 in July 1939 to 1,643 in 1945. The BBC became a corporate member in 1942. There was a special subscription rate for members of the armed forces of 10s 6d: the full rate, including all pamphlets and periodicals, was £1 5s.

With shortage of staff, materials and money, with all its facilities curtailed, with public interest diverted to matters of – at least temporarily – greater moment, it was inevitably a period of marking time for the BFI. If asked what it did during the war it might at best be able to reply, with the Abbé Sieyès during the Great Terror, *"J'ai vécu"*. In all the circumstances, even this may be considered something of an achievement.

The following three years also found the Institute doing little more than ticking over as the country slowly and painfully tried to drag itself back to something like normal. Olwen Vaughan resigned in June 1945, after ten years, because, she said, "of the BFI's increasing concern with the educational rather than the artistic side of the cinema." She subsequently became film officer with UNRAA. In September Lord Chattisham died suddenly and was succeeded by Patrick Gordon Walker. A suggestion was made by Sir Thomas Moore that the Institute should carry on the work of the Ministry of Information when it was wound up, and should commission and distribute films of Britain. The Institute, it was said was not performing a sufficiently important role in public affairs. Mr Aidan Crawley stated that he had recently seen *Fame is the Spur* (1947, directed by Roy Boulting) on board the *Queen Elizabeth* and doubted the advisability of showing such a film on a British liner to a predominantly American audience. What action could the BFI take? Tactfully the reply was given – none. Well, what steps could be taken to ensure that only "good quality" films were shown on board British ships? The film in question told the story of a liberal English politician who refused to sacrifice his ideals. Its screening in mid-Atlantic seems to have had no deleterious effect on Anglo-American relations.

More constructively, the National Film Library protested against the suppression of Thorold Dickinson's fine version of Patrick Hamilton's play *Gaslight* (1939) by an American company producing a remake. Such protests, which should most certainly be made whether they have any immediate effect or not, were to be raised on future occasions against similar sacrifices of works of artistic merit to commercial expediency, notably in regard to Marcel Carné's *Le Jour se Lève*.

In 1947 an unusual and enterprising festival of Czech films was held at the New Gallery Cinema, Regent Street, with the encouragement and support of the Home Office. Patrons included Ernest Bevin, Herbert Morrison and Sir Stafford Cripps, whose interest may have been political rather than aesthetic. The season was attended by twenty-five Czech delegates representing all sides of the film industry. It included the famous underground movement film *Men Without Wings*, and was later repeated in Glasgow.

In the same year a committee was set up under the chairmanship of the pioneer producer and director Cecil Hepworth to look into the possibilities of publishing a comprehensive and authoritative history of the British film, which up to that time was poorly chronicled. The first volume, by Rachael Low and Roger Manvell, covering the years 1896–1906, appeared in 1948, the second, from 1906 to 1914, in 1949 and a third, 1914–18, in 1951. Thereafter the series was suspended for a long period, owing to Miss Low's absence, but she has recently completed a fourth volume covering the period 1918–29. By the time the series is completed the British cinema should be one of the best documented in the world.

Additional premises were leased at 164 Shaftesbury Avenue, the first Governor's meeting being held there in March 1948. The four-thousandth member was accepted in the same month, 2,112 being active on the register.

3. *1948 to 1955*

In April 1948 occurred the second of the three most significant events in the history of the BFI to date – the first being the founding of the NFL, later the Archive, and the third the opening of the National Film Theatre. This was the issue of the Radcliffe Report on the future constitution and scope of the Institute. The way for the preparation of such a report had been cleared by the formation of two organisations which were to relieve the Institute of certain of its former responsibilities: the National Committee for Visual Aids in Education in 1946 to take over the use of films in schools, and the British Film Academy in 1947 to serve as a meeting ground for artists and technicians.

At the end of 1947 a committee was appointed by Herbert

Morrison, Lord President of the Council, to enquire into the BFI. The Chairman, who gave the Report its name, was Sir Cyril J. Radcliffe, later Lord Radcliffe, and the members were Sir Ernest Pooley, Charles Robertson, Sir Stephen Tallents, Norman Wilson, and the film critic Miss Dilys Powell. Miss J. H. Lidderdale acted as secretary. The importance of this Report and its recommendations cannot be over-emphasised. It radically altered the aims and objectives of the Institute, started it off on a fresh footing, and injected new life into a somewhat tired and lethargic body. It first outlined the Institute's activities to date under three main heads:

"(a) It has established a National Film Library in which are preserved films selected to show how the art of the film has developed and to serve as a record of contemporary manners . . .

(b) It has started an information section intended to deal with enquiries over a wide field and with correspondence and work in connection with similar activities overseas . . .

(c) It has promoted appreciation of film as a form of art and the specialised use of film – largely in the field of education – through its publications and by lecturers, by summer schools and courses, and by the encouragement of allied societies."

It summarised the financial position:

"The grant from the Cinematograph Fund averaged under £9,000 a year from the date of the Institute's foundation until 1944 when it jumped to £14,000, rose to £18,000 the following year and jumped again to £22,100 for 1946. For 1947 it was fixed at £31,500 to remain at this figure for 1948 and 1949. Until quite recently, therefore, the funds available to the Institute have been extremely modest when viewed in the light of the activities it was designed to undertake and such funds have always been granted on a yearly basis."

It recommended for the future three executive responsibilities:

(a) the administration of the National Film Library;

(b) the conduct of a first-class information service;

(c) the development of a central and regional organisation to promote appreciation of the film art and new or extended uses for the cinema.

The most significant paragraph in the Report, and the one that reshaped the course of the Institute and fundamentally shifted its emphasis was the conclusion that it should in future "encourage the development of the art of the film, promote its use as a record of contemporary life and manners and foster public appreciation and study of it from these points of view." As a corollary to this: "Responsibility for promoting the use of film in education, whether as a visual aid or as a subject of appreciation, will in future lie with the National Committee for Visual Aids in Education so far as concerns local education authorities. But such authorities should look to the Institute as at least one of the sources from which their teachers can obtain expert instruction, advice and material in matters of film appreciation."

From this time forwards the BFI could see its way more clearly before it, and the acquisition of a film theatre of its own, in which the public, as members, could for the first time see films under its auspices, became an obvious and urgent essential. By a piece of fortunate timing, arrangements for the Festival of Britain, of which the BFI was a constituent body, were getting under way. The Institute was already co-operating in the setting up of a cinema on the site of the Exhibition wherein would be demonstrated the latest technical developments in film, such as 3-D and multi-stereophonic sound, and in closed circuit television. From this grew the idea of a permanent repertory theatre for films – the germ of the National Film Theatre. The Telekinema, as it was called, was retained after the closure of the Exhibition – after some difficult negotiations with the then London County Council – until the NFT was moved to its own building on South Bank in 1957.

The effect of the new policy and the establishment of a theatre for members (i.e. the public) can be seen concisely and vividly in the numbers on the register for the following ten years:

	Full Members	Associate Members	
1948	2,118		
1949	2,297		
1950	2,266		
1951	2,173		
1952	2,015	92	(Opening of the Telekinema as the NFT)

	Full Members	*Associate Members*	
1953	4,622	13,353	
1954	6,450	17,511	
1955	6,764	18,709	
1956	6,539	21,008	
1957	7,019	27,216	(Opening of the new NFT on South Bank)
1958	7,739	32,390	

In May 1952 applications for membership were the highest in the history of the Institute. In 1953 a proposal for a half-guinea guest membership lasting three months was approved.

Following the Radcliffe Report two major changes in the Institute's officers took place. Cecil King, proprietor of the *Daily Mirror*, became Chairman of the Board of Governors, with a mandate from Herbert Morrison to reorganise the Institute on the lines of the Report, and Denis Forman succeeded Oliver Bell as Director.

At the time of his appointment Denis Forman knew very little about the BFI but a good deal about films. He had been working for John Grierson at the Crown Film Unit for some time, and it was Grierson who advised him to apply for the new post. "My brief," he says, "was to think again from scratch. It was an exciting prospect. I saw three parallel necessities:

"(a) greatly to enlarge the membership and thus provide additional finance by increased subscriptions. We had a grant in aid from the Lord Privy Seal and a slice still of the Cinematograph Fund, but this was diminishing. We had to make our way by our own efforts.

"(b) to obtain a public building to show films. There was not a small cinema in London which we had not considered before the Telekinema came along, including old bombed-out buildings in the Tottenham Court Road. Most of those available had to be turned down on account of cost. The Academy in Oxford Street came on offer, but this would have meant taking over the whole building, which we could not afford.

"(c) to enliven and streamline *Sight and Sound*."

In all these projects he was to receive the greatest help from the

Secretary, Robert Camplin, "a tower of strength", who reorganised the whole administration of the Institute's affairs.

But the change of policy also entailed, in the first six months of his term, a less pleasant duty, one which Forman describes as a "traumatic experience". The Radcliffe Committee had stated in its report: "It is clear that adjustments in staff will be necessary as the result of our recommendations and we regard this as one of the first matters for consideration by the new Board of Governors." Forman says, "We had, quite simply, not the right staff for the new projects, and one of my first jobs was to make the unavoidable changes. A lot of nice, dedicated people had to go – saying goodbye to them and replacing them was the hardest thing I had to do." The change was not only reflected in the internal membership. The noticeable drop in applications from the public in 1950–52 before the first NFT opened was in all probability due to the fact that older members, interested in the original policies, were falling out before the theatre brought in the new. A similar drop in full membership during 1955–56 may well have been caused by the knowledge that the lease of the Telekinema was running out and the future of the NFT uncertain.

New terms of membership were offered in 1950:
(a) a general subscription of £2 2s to include *Sight and Sound*, the *Monthly Film Bulletin* and the use of various informational facilities, and (b) a special membership of £3 10s, to include the repertory season of films then being held at the Institut Français (see the chapter on the National Film Archive), the use of the private cinema and the television viewing room, receipt of publications, and membership of London film societies at reduced rates. The special rate was dropped after a comparatively short period. In 1952, when the Telekinema was taken over, an associate membership of 5s was opened.

Generally speaking, the accent in the new Institute was on youth. The founding of the Experimental Film Production Fund, later the Film Production Board, which followed hard on the acquisition of a place where films could be shown, enabled young film-makers of promise to take the first steps towards entering the industry. The new editorial board of *Sight and Sound* consisted of young writers and critics with new standards and new viewpoints, "That," says Forman, "is what made things hum."

Relations with the trade during this period of change and expansion blew, as they had often blown hitherto, hot and cold. "There was," Forman remarks, "always a misplaced fear from exhibitors that the National Film Theatre was depriving, or was about to deprive, commercial houses of their audience. In actual fact, of course, the types of programme were wholly different. Apart from this, any raising in the general level of appreciation could only benefit the cinema as a whole – a fact which the industry eventually came to realise. Sir Henry French, Director of the British Film Producers Association was at this time also one of the Governors of the BFI and on more than one occasion supported the Institute against the wild-cat members of the Association."

A cat *was*, however, set among the pigeons by an article in *Sight and Sound* (April 1950) written by 'Frank Enley' a pseudonym for Gavin Lambert, in which he savagely attacked the British police film *The Blue Lamp* (in which Dock Green's Dixon was germinated), with side swipes at certain aspects of the country's productions as a whole. In retrospect it became clear that the film was not without considerable importance, and it gave a great fillip to the British industry at the time. Understandably, the latter were annoyed at the torrent of abuse, but Cecil King upheld the right of criticism and said that the publication was fulfilling its proper function. Criticism of *Sight and Sound*'s coverage of the British cinema has persisted, in varying degrees of intensity, to this day.

4. *1955 to 1964*

In 1955 Denis Forman was succeeded by James Quinn, who remained as Director until 1964.* Whereas Forman's period was one of revitalisation and revaluation following the Radcliffe Report, much of James Quinn's energies were directed towards expansion, and a struggle to retain Governmental support. In his book he writes:

* Cecil King was succeeded as Chairman in 1952 by S. C. Roberts, master of Pembroke College Cambridge. He in turn was followed in 1956 by Sylvester Gates, Chairman of the Bank of West Africa, and Deputy Chairman of Westminster Bank, who remained with the BFI for over eight years and is still spoken of with great warmth by all who worked with him.

"Between 1954 and 1958 the Government's grant rose steadily, if modestly, and always exceeded the Institute's earnings, but thereafter until 1965 the rate of increase from public funds was much less and scarcely rose at all between 1958 and 1960. In contrast, the institute's earnings continued to rise sharply for most of the time between 1960 and 1964 and invariably exceeded its grant from the Government. One further point should be made in any assessment, in money terms, of the Institute's development. This concerns the Institute's growth in relation to Government expenditure on the arts in general.

"The Treasury publication *Government and the Arts 1958–64* shows a marked advance in the Government's attitude towards subsidy for the arts, other than the film, in recent years. As the British Film Institute *Report 1965* points out, 'The Arts Council grant now stands at three times the figure of six years ago. Covent Garden's grant for opera for 1964–65 amounts to just over a million pounds. The cost of National Art Galleries and Museums has increased by 150 per cent.' By comparison, the Institute's grant, it was calculated, had increased by only 62 per cent, and still accounted for less than one per cent of the total allocated by the Government under the Arts and Sciences vote."

Soon the Treasury was considering closing down all Institute activities excepting the Film Archive, allowing that the NFT should continue, if it could, under its own steam. The reason? "In a period of retrenchment, we cannot afford this sort of thing" – representing the contempt with which, in certain sections of the community, the film was still regarded.

Yet this was at a time when the Institute was represented on outside committees of such bodies as the Arts Council, the British Standards Institution, the Bureau Internationale de la Recherche Historique Cinématographique, the Joint Council for Education through Art, the National Council of Women, the National Council of Social Services, the Royal Anthropological Society Film Committee, the Royal Institute of British Architects, the Scientific Film Association*, and UNESCO; when the Foreign

* Founded in 1942 to promote a wider use of films in science: amalgamated in 1967 with the British Industrial Film Association and renamed the British Industrial and Scientific Film Association.

Office was in the habit of "showing off" the NFT and BFI premises to foreign delegates; when organisations such as the Commonwealth Relations Office, the Central Office of Information and the British Council were anxious to engage the services of BFI lecturers overseas.

Sections of the press also joined in attacks. In 1954 *The People* published an article denouncing the Institute for misusing a Government grant in aid to provide cheap seats for its members at the NFT, and Lord Beaverbrook's *Evening Standard* curled a righteous lip at the thought of public money financing a luxury cinema – when not a penny of such money was going into it.

In the face of this hostile attitude from Government and press (and to some extent the industry also), the BFI sought by every available means to bring home to the Government the importance of its work. In practice this was done in three ways:

(a) by bringing the Institute's activities before the general public at a popular level;

(b) by extending the sphere and scope of its influence internationally;

(c) by raising its standards on the scholarly and academic side by achieving general recognition of the film as an art form and establishing university lecturcships.

The first of these aims entailed securing the continuity of the NFT and led to the inauguration of the London Film Festival: it also included the promotion of exhibitions and other publicity projects. The most important of the latter was the 'Sixty Years of Cinema' Exhibition presented jointly by the BFI and the *Observer* newspaper in the spring and summer of 1956. This was based on a very successful display on similar lines arranged in Paris by the Cinémathèque Française. Finding themselves altogether without the means to mark, even in the smallest way, a significant year in the cinema's history, the BFI persuaded the *Observer* to finance the transporting and mounting of the French exhibition in London.

Directed by Richard Buckle, it was sited in a temporary building near the National Gallery and consisted mainly of displays of film stills and other photographs, books, and technical equipment, together with daily showings of film classics presented by the NFT. Admission was 2s 6d and 3s 6d, cinema extra.

c

Reactions to the exhibition were by no means uniformly favourable. Lindsay Anderson, for instance, strongly attacked it in an article entitled "Stand Up! Stand Up!" published in *Sight and Sound*, in the course of which he referred to the "orthodox, unadventurous choice of stills, selected on conventional, academic and chronological principles, disposed in a series of sophisticated decors, which tended to 'kill' rather than set off the material on display." Despite imperfections, however, many of which were undoubtedly due to the fact that the facilities available were not really adequate for its scope, the 'Sixty Years of Cinema' Exhibition certainly accomplished part of its purpose. It was attended by some 200,000 people, and sent full and associate Institute membership up at a time when it usually declined.

The following year saw another important innovation in the shape of the first London Film Festival (see p. 129) for which the *Sunday Times* stood in relation to the BFI much as the *Observer* had done with the exhibition. The festival was closely linked with the second element of the BFI's strategy, the building up of influence and contacts abroad. In addition to the international festival various foreign film seasons were held at the NFT, in conjunction with the embassies of the countries concerned. Famous directors from four foreign countries were present at the opening of the new National Film Theatre in 1957. Quinn himself went abroad to meet film-makers – arranging for the supply of films and other joint enterprises – with the object of bringing the Foreign Office and other government departments to a realisation of the BFI's value and prestige abroad. One of the most successful of these was an extensive lecture tour in India and Pakistan under the auspices of the Commonwealth Relations Office. Another, to Venice to serve on the festival jury, resulted in an unexpected bonus for the Archive, when Luchino Visconti presented him with a copy of *La Terra Trema*.

In the third category came the creation in 1960 of a university lectureship in film at the Slade School of Art. This, though it attracted less public attention than other activities, was perhaps the most significant innovation of all. In the customary absence of government support all the funds required had to be raised from "outside" sources. Eventually a total amount of £25,000 was advanced or guaranteed under deed of covenant for an experimental period of five years by the Film Production Association of Great Britain, the Associated British Picture Corporation and the J. Arthur Rank Charity Trust. The introduction of the lectureship to the Slade had the whole-hearted support of Sir William Coldstream, Head of the Slade School and from 1964 Chairman of the Governors of the BFI. Thorold Dickinson, the film director whose productions include *Gaslight*, 1939; *Next of Kin*, 1941; and *The Queen of Spades*, 1948) was appointed Lecturer, a position he still holds, together with two post-graduate research students. Quinn writes, "No hard and fast scheme was laid down for the new department, and within the limitations of a minute budget the lecturer had a free hand. . . . Although it had always been envisaged that the emphasis would be on the critical and aesthetic aspects of film it was accepted that there would need to be some facilities for film-making by the students. It was also accepted that the department should seek to provide a service for other facilities in the University, and from the outset programmes of films on many subjects, including history and literature, have been arranged by the film lecturer in collaboration with the departments concerned." The lectureship was given professional status in 1967.

Amid these large schemes, under the shadow of governmental lack of interest, life went on. The NFT withdrew its coffee service in 1961, but served drinks. Receipts at the theatre were above average.

The Cinematograph Exhibitors' Association voiced objections to the theatre's attempts to popularise its programmes.

The Archive Stills Collection had a windfall when it acquired the entire collection of the defunct magazine *Picture Show*, some 400,000 photographs.

The German General Spiedel threatened a libel action because the Institute had allowed the Plato Film Company to screen *Operation Teutonic Sword*, a documentary allegedly based on his career and directed by Andrew and Annelie Thorndike. The Company hired the NFT to press show the film in November 1959. The storm blew over, but it was suggested at a board meeting that future contracts should provide indemnity in such contingencies. There was more trouble the following year over an invitation sent to Leni Riefenstahl, the brilliant but notorious director of the Nazi spectacles *Triumph of the Will* and *Olympiade 1936* and, in pre-Hitlerian days, of the magnificent 'mountain' films *The White Hell of Pitz Palu* and *The Blue Light*. When it was learnt that she had been invited to lecture at the NFT complaints, some of them violent, were received from numerous quarters, including the German Embassy. One gentleman went so far as to smash with his fist a photograph of Miss Riefenstahl in the club room – a scene which must have astonished that lively but generally amicable meeting place. The view taken by Stanley Reed, then in charge of the NFT, was that opportunities should be afforded to members to hear anyone of distinction in the world of the cinema, regardless of political affinities. "Satan himself is welcome at the NFT," he said, "provided he makes good pictures." Eventually, however, concern for public safety, which it was felt might have been endangered by a clash between neo-fascists and left-wingers, caused the invitation to be withdrawn. Both films have since been shown on several occasions, to packed houses. Similar objections were raised in 1969 when a season on 'The Film and Nazi Germany' was in the process of being planned. At first a decision was made to cancel the programme, but finally it was shown the following year, without noticeable protest.*

In 1960 the Institute after a long search and protracted negotiations, acquired larger and more comfortable premises, though it was not to be long before even these were to prove inadequate. It has never yet achieved its ambition to house all its offices in under half-a-dozen widely separated buildings. The move to 81 Dean Street, Soho, took place in June of that year. "The scruffy building in Shaftesbury Avenue with no reading rooms, no public rooms and precious little room for anything else," to quote James Quinn, "was left without regret. We were at last able to persuade the Government to take over the building in Dean Street and install the BFI on a very favourable lease. They were, of course, also acquiring a very valuable property for themselves." Rent and

* "This particular problem, the extent to which one should have regard to current political opinion, still causes concern on occasion. In the autumn of 1970 a short Algerian season had been planned to screen a number of exceptionally interesting films, but this was cancelled because of the recent kidnappings and the possible risk to the public from extremist demonstrations" – Stanley Reed.

rates (in 1959/60) amounted to £15,000 for Dean Street as against £10,000 for the Shaftesbury Avenue premises.

Two projects of the period which met with less success than those outlined above were each connected with television. In its yearly survey *Outlook* (1965) the BFI summarised its attitude to the new medium in the early sixties: "The Institute sees its functions as an expanding one. Indeed, it could hardly do otherwise at a time when the uses of the film are themselves undergoing such rapid change and development. In particular, it has in recent years made the advance into television, and in 1961 the Objects Clause of the Institute's Memorandum of Association was altered, with Treasury assent, to take account of this new concern. There has been occasional criticism of this venture into television, on the grounds that the Institute was in some way betraying its original loyalties. From all practical points of view, however, the move was not only logical but so inevitable as hardly to need theoretical justification. . . . At many points . . . television and film overlap; and if the Institute had tried to ignore television it would have been placing itself in a position not only impossible but ridiculous." The first step was the issue of *Contrast*, a quarterly magazine designed to "provide comment on television programmes and on trends and developments in television." The Institute itself contributed no funds towards the publication as the Government insisted that it should be self-supporting, but the BBC and Granada Television each contributed £12,000 for a trial run over a three-year period. In the event, *Contrast* lasted nearly five years, but in 1966, despite the fact that it reduced its format, and that its editor at that time, David Robinson, gave his services free of charge, its sales could not maintain it any longer on an economic basis and it was closed down. The fact that publication coincided with that of a television company magazine may have been a contributing factor to the lack of public response, as may the fact that, with so ephemeral a medium, a quarterly magazine could only refer to actual programmes which were long past and unlikely to be seen again. Even in a daily paper, television criticism, unless it is referring to a series or recurrent programme, has an obsequial air as of words spoken over a dear – or damned – departed. Television has yet to find an aesthetic that can be discussed on its own terms. As Stanley Reed, in charge of publications at that time, put it, "the fundamental reason for the magazine's failure was that people are not interested in 'television'. They are interested in the things that are on television, but not in 'television' as they might be in 'theatre', 'music' or 'cinema'. Film is an art in its own right, television is a medium of transmission. The medium may be put to excellent use, but it's the subject matter, the content, that people want to know about, not the artistic quality of its presentation. Almost the entire readership of *Contrast* was professional, workers in the medium anxious to read about their own and their colleagues' contributions. The general public just didn't want to know about it."

The other attempt to bring the BFI into closer relationship with the new medium was the Festival of World Television organised at the NFT in 1963. This was a complicated undertaking, requiring a vast amount of planning. No extra financial support was received from the Government, the money being supplied by the BBC, ITA and Independent Television companies, who each put up £2,000; help was also received from the makers of television equipment. The object was to show, on closed circuit television, the best programmes of world television, and eventually to set up an annual festival something on the lines of the London Film Festival. However, considerable difficulty was encountered in obtaining sufficient material, and the occasion did not arouse the interest that was hoped for among the Institute's members. An additional drawback was the insistence by the television companies concerned that the programmes should be transmitted on small screens at the moment they were being projected on the full-size cinema screen. Consequently television sets were placed about the theatre around which groups of people gathered, watching the large screen and the small ones at the same time. It was, says Stanley Reed, not a happy compromise, though the insistence of the television authorities was perfectly understandable because much of the material which was altogether acceptable on a small screen became ludicrous when seen on a large one. It was disappointing, also, that though the festival attracted a lot of favourable attention both at home and abroad, it was almost totally ignored by the regular television press critics.

As a result of all this, plans for future Festivals were dropped.

In 1964, towards the end of the period we have been considering, a graph was drawn up showing that the peak number of members plus associates had been reached in 1961. Thenceforward the associate total had declined but the full membership continued to grow steadily. "Deteriorating condition of the South Bank" was held responsible for the associate decline. Figures in early 1965 showed totals of 10,275 full, 20,376 associate, as compared with 10,123 and 25,041 in 1961.

During a period of governmental lack of interest, of threats of closure and continuing financial stringency, the BFI had widely expanded its sphere of influence, undertaken numerous and often highly complex projects – some successful, others less so – and finished up with a total membership of over 35,000.

5. *1964 to 1970*

The year 1964 saw the return to power of a Labour Government, and for the BFI a new Chairman and a new Director. A survey of the Institute's role in the mid-'60s was given, under the heading "A Policy of Risk", in the publication *Outlook 1965*. After referring to the current position in the various departments, the report continues: "Behind all this diversification of activity must be some philosophical conception of the Institute's role. Public attitudes to the cinema change; the cinema itself changes; and the function of an organisation like the Institute in the mid-'60s is bound to be rather different from anything envisaged by its founders in the early '30s. Since then the cinema has won the immense audiences of the war years, and lost it again to affluence, television and the motor-car. Film-going in this country is no longer a habit, good or bad, but a selective process. Film-making has become increasingly diversified, with new countries moving into production, and artists working in conditions of independence hardly possible during the disciplined days of the great studios.

"The concern of the Institute has always been with the public rather than the film-maker, the consumer rather than the creator. Only through its Experimental Fund* is it able to give direct

* Now known as the Film Production Board.

encouragement to the artist, and then only on a miniscule scale. But by collecting and transmitting not only films but information about films, by ensuring that the fragile stuff of this impermanent art is preserved, and by endeavouring to play its part in the general raising of critical sights, it can also hope indirectly to serve the artists as well as the public. The position of the cinema is no different from that of any of the other arts, and the principles at issue remain constant: the right of the artist on occasion to disregard the question of profit, to explore beyond the safe confines of the commercially acceptable, and the right of interested audiences to see his work."

Responsibility for financing the BFI was transferred from the Treasury to the Department of Education and Science.

The new Chairman was Sir William Coldstream, Professor of Fine Art at the Slade School, London, and formerly deputy chairman of the Arts Council. Stanley Reed, the new Director, is the first to have worked previously with the BFI. At one time a schoolmaster in London's East End, he joined the Institute in 1950 as a lecturer. Later he took over the Distribution Library and the Central Agency. In 1956 he was considering leaving to take on a job with Ilford, Ltd. the photographic firm, when he was asked to remain as Secretary. He supervised the publications department, and later the NFT. He had, in fact, as he says, a substantial chunk of departments. With Ernest Lindgren, Curator of the Archive, he became a deputy director, and on the retirement of James Quinn took over the directorship.

Reed's main interest has always been in the widening of critical interest in the film among the popular audience, particularly by direct teaching in schools. "Even when I began teaching in West Ham during the late '20s," he says, "I found that the surest way of making communication with the children was to discuss with them the films they had seen. Their interest in and enthusiasm for the cinema was boundless, and I felt then that this interest should be encouraged to continue and develop at higher levels." One of his first projects on joining the Institute was to set up an education department, the policy of which, based on the Radcliffe Report, was to concentrate on "promoting the appreciation of film as an art and as entertainment, leaving the use of film as a visual aid in

the teaching of other subjects, to the various specialist bodies."
This is so obviously an important part of the organisation's
functions that it is surprising (particularly in view of the establishment in 1960 of the Slade Professorship, the long-standing existence of the Summer Schools, and the lecture service) that it took
as long as sixteen years since the Radcliffe Report for such a
department to be set up. In this connection Reed edited a booklet
entitled *Critics' Choice*, consisting of collected reviews of current
films by a panel of established critics and linked with the NFT
programme bulletins, and also produced *Film Guide*. Now discontinued, this was a wall sheet designed for use in schools, showing what films were showing during any particular week, the
names of the cinemas, and a few critical comments. Several
hundred London schools subscribed to the monthly issues.

Apart from the Eduation Department, Reed set himself, on
taking office, four principal aims:
(a) to find a permanent home for the preservation of the Archive.
(b) to restart the Film Production Board after its lapse through
lack of funds.
(c) to develop the activities of the BFI outside London.
(d) to establish a national film school.

The Institute now found a good friend in the new Minister for
Arts, Miss Jennie Lee. After paying several visits to the offices and
the NFT, and attending Governors' Meetings, Miss Lee voiced
her appreciation of the work being done and promised to seek
governmental support on all four objectives. As will be seen in the
relevant sections of this book, within eighteen months the first
three had been accomplished.

The National Film School has proved a harder nut to crack, and
plans have matured only slowly. The idea of forming a school to
train future film-makers – and film-viewers – is as old as the
Institute itself. But the even older prejudices die hard. Teach
people – with public money – to work in 'the pictures'? The
attitude that the cinema is a frivolous time-waster, unworthy of
serious consideration or of being considered an art, is still – despite
all the evidence to the contrary – an unconscionable time a-dying.
It is an attitude which, to their discredit, *certain* sections of the
industry – with their indiscriminate policy of grinding-on-regard-

less continuous performances, parades of nut-and-ices sellers sometimes during the showing of the main feature itself, film-slashing to fit programmes (or obtain time for commercials), blantantly cheap and sensational advertising methods – have done little to counteract and much to encourage. Thus it took many years of effort before the idea of a school showed any signs of maturing, but eventually a committee was set up under the chairmanship of Lord Lloyd, a governor of the Institute, and similar schools in Poland, Italy and elsewhere were visited and studied. A decision had been made earlier that the BFI should not itself run such a school, but that, once established, it should become an independent concern, though able to call when necessary on all the Institute facilities available. Even then the scheme was not without its opponents. In 1968 it was pointed out that only two film technicians had entered the industry during the past two or three years from schools then existing. Practically all the remainder went into television. However, when the committee's recommendations were submitted to Miss Lee they were accepted by the Government, and a director, Colin Young, has since been appointed with an office at the NFT. In an interview with Terence Kelly for the autumn 1970 number of *Sight and Sound* Young described his conception of the ideal film school as "open-minded, undogmatic, socially responsible and closely connected to contemporary life." He referred to the complaints of present-day film-makers that they work in the dark and lack mutual contact, and listed the advantages to be gained from a school. "One is the opportunity to see a lot of films in a short period in a fairly controlled situation where they can make maximum use of having seen them. The second is to have been in the company of people who had precisely similar problems to theirs, approaching them more or less systematically. And the third is having the access to equipment made much simpler." On the selection of teachers, he remarked, "Our problem will be to find technicians sympathetic to the idea that absolutely nothing has yet been proven about the way technique works in creating a good film, with minds completely open to the idea that every technique that has been invented can be reinvented or rediscovered or rejected." The question now remains whether the present member under the

Conservative Government, Lord Eccles, will continue the support so far given. If so, it is hoped that the long-deferred hope for a national school of film will have become a reality by the autumn of 1971.

A second large-scale exhibition of the cinema was held in the autumn of 1970 at the Round House, Chalk Farm. Sponsored by the National Film Archive and the *Sunday Times*, who put up all the necessary finance, it was a survey of the seventy-five years since the Lumière brothers gave the first public demonstration of their Cinématographie in Paris. Entitled 'Cinema City', it was designed by Emile Gambia, with George Perry (assistant editor of the *Sunday Times* and Colin Ford (deputy curator of the National Film Archive) as directors. In his foreword to the catalogue Lord Thomson of Fleet wrote: "In my younger days it was often hard to get people to take the movies seriously as an art. Happily, that debate is long over and now their contribution to the quality of critical thought is acknowledged. Yet the movies are also a great industry, albeit one that like my own has in recent years met with monumental problems. Cinema City is a celebration of the first seventy-five years of the cinema, a tribute to those pioneers at the end of the nineteenth century who gave us this wonderful invention. It is also a joyful recollection of what the movies are about and a reminder to us all that film is a fragile medium deserving of protection and preservation."

The actual exhibition section was divided into twelve parts dealing with different themes – technical history, epic, comedy, thriller, western, musical, etc. – and concluding with student films from the London Film School and the University of Bristol. Visitors made a sort of circular tour through darkened rooms in each of which a programme of film-clips and stills was projected lasting about seven minutes. The result was inevitably scrappy, and probably confusing to the uninformed or casual visitor, but passing through the rooms in succession afforded a surprisingly impressive view of the sheer scope of the film medium. The main attraction, however, was the huge auditorium, wherein four to five complete films were shown daily, at intervals from 11 a.m. to 11 p.m., and where celebrities gave interviews about their work. The range of subjects was wide, from early silents (including

Harold Lloyd's *Kid Brother*, which he brought over personally, and Chaplain's *The Circus* – neither of which had been seen in London for over thirty years) to others not yet publicly released in Britain.

Cinema City was launched by a charity première of *Catch-22* (directed by Mike Nichols) in the presence of Princess Margaret, all proceeds from which went to the Archive. The official opening was performed by Princess Alexandra, with Harold Lloyd, who had flown from California for the event, as special guest. The choice of the Round House was perhaps an unfortunate one, not only on account of its inaccessibility. Originally a railway engine storage and maintenance building, a general atmosphere of smoke, coal, stone and iron still overshadows it, and its vast murk is not a cheerful setting for such an exhibition. In one respect, however, Cinema City was an unqualified success, and that was in the impressive array of film personalities who appeared in order to give talks or interviews. This included Richard Attenborough, Richard Burton and Elizabeth Taylor, Gene Kelly, Eartha Kitt, Shirley Maclaine, Colleen Moore, Peter Sellers, Omar Sharif, Cavalcanti, John Frankenheimer, Peter Hall, Mervyn LeRoy, Joseph Losey, Louis Malle, Norman Mailer, Roman Polanski, Michael Powell, John Schlesinger, Lotte Reiniger, King Vidor, Luchino Visconti, William Wyler, Franco Zeffirelli, Robert Krasker, Walter Lassally, John Addison, Dmitri Tiomkin, George Axelrod, Robert Bolt and, last but by no means least, the then Secretary of the British Board of Film Censors, John Trevelyan. On the last day a unique auction was held in the auditorium, independently of the Exhibition, of a large mass of vintage posters, stills and magazine. By far the highest bid was that of £80 for 56 postcards of Greta Garbo: 42 8 inches by 10 inches portraits of Claudette Colbert raised £4 by comparison, and 20 of Clara Bow brought in £8: 300 postcards of stage stars brought in £6 10s, in contrast to £17 for about the same number of cinema stars of the '20s and '30s: 45 photographs of hands and feet, gloves and shoes of pre-1940 stars went for £5 10s, and 75 of stars eating (the food was not specified) for £3 10s. All tastes were catered for.

A total of some 25,000 people visited Cinema City during its run: 147 full-length feature films were shown, eighteen of which were the first British or world screenings. It cost about £35,000 to set up, and the box office returns were under £9,500, resulting in a loss to the *Sunday Times* of over £25,000 against an estimated loss of £15,000. Even so, George Perry claims that it was a success "because it proved the point that people want to go to the cinema, some coming from as far away as Liverpool." Attendances were hit to some extent by the unfortunate coincidence of a newspaper strike, with resulting limitations on publicity. And it is presumably encouraging to know that people will travel as far to see a £35,000 cinema exhibition as they will to watch a football match.

Any organisation run, in part at least, on public money, offering an open membership, and concerned with a combination of the artistic and the commercial, is particularly open to critical attack. It is, indeed, an indication of their significance and vitality that this should be so, and the BFI has had its fair share, interior and exterior, weighty and trivial. Board meetings are often lively, with complaints and dissension healthily aired rather than permitted to fester in secret: there was a famous legendary (and undocumented) occasion when one Institute member poured a glass of beer over another's head – conjuring up visions of Fellini-esque orgies.

Often it is a case of steering between Scylla and Charybdis, and falling victim to both. In 1969 numerous complaints were received about the inclusion of New Cinema Club booklets in the NFT programme brochures sent to members, on account of their allegedly pornographic content, and similar indignation was aroused by some of the material shown during the Underground Film Season in 1970. "Some of the films had quality," says Reed, "but there was undoubtedly a fringe of pornography. We decided there should be no censorship, and were hauled over the coals for it. Had we attempted (then or at any other time) to impose such a censorship we should have been attacked with equal vehemence. We will be accused of being (a) too esoteric, (b) too popular, (c) too wide-ranging, (d) too narrowly bound – sometimes all at the same time. Criticism of this nature is inevitable when, for instance, as in the case of the Film Production Board, we are forced to discriminate between the projects of aspiring film-makers, deciding to finance Mr X's film but not Mr Y's, and when reviews appear in *Sight and Sound* or the *Monthly Film Bulletin* which do not look altogether favourably on films made by the Institute's own professional members. This is both perfectly understandable, and quite unavoidable."

A major attack was launched in 1968 with the appearance in the press of an open letter addressed to Miss Jennie Lee. Drawn up by David Adnopoz, Jonathan Hansen, Maurice Hatton and Stacy Waddy, it accused the BFI of apathy and atrophy, and of being unable any longer to "cope with the needs of a new and internationally orientated generation of film-makers." The words "internationally orientated" read oddly in conjunction with the periodic accusation that the Institute does not devote sufficient emphasis to the films of its own country. The letter charged also that it lacked breadth of taste – which was described as that of a tight coterie. The Archive was condemned for its policy of passive preservation for posterity. "Posterity is now", declared the writers, adopting Humpty Dumpty's method of making words mean whatever you choose them to mean, regardless of sense. Impenetrability, indeed.

The letter went on to put forward in detail points for an alternative organisation to be entitled Cinetec International London, with somewhat optimistic suggestions regarding the allocation of funds. A formidable list of signatures was appended in support, including Tony Richardson, Clive Donner, Paul Rotha, Susannah York, John Schlesinger, Sean Kenney, Joan Littlewood, Tony Garnett and Donovan Winter.

The Institute was defended by Edgar Anstey, then a governor, who pointed out that finance was simply not equal to the enormous amount of work the Institute had to deal with. "There is a lot more that it could do. But as a body the present governors are well capable of getting it done in the fullness of time." From Miss Lee came the following (considerably briefer) open reply, which received less publicity than the original letter: "Thank you for sending me a copy of the open letter to me that had already appeared in the Press. But don't you think this is a rather odd way of going about things? I certainly do, more especially as excellent positive suggestions for improving and extending the work of the British Film Institute, many of them very like your own, have repeatedly and insistently been brought to my notice by the Board of Governors. I in turn have not been backward in discussing their view with my Treasury colleagues. So what about a little fair play? Why attack the Governors for not doing what they want to do but lack the means to do, even though Government aid to the Institute has been trebled since 1963?

"I am particularly grateful to both the Governors and staff for the high priority given to making films of quality available in many parts of the country where the work of the Institute was formerly unknown. Twenty regional film theatres have been established and more are planned. In addition, much needed improvements have been made in the building up and re-housing of the National Film Archive. There has unfortunately not been much over to help young film-makers; I am also very well aware how keenly the Governors feel about the present limited availability of the Archive. These problems must be overcome as soon as more funds can be found.

"On their present budget, I do not see how the Governors could better arrange their priorities. What do you think they should do? Cut the good work being done in the regions? Cut the work of the Archive? If not, then what?"

The letter was taken seriously by the Director and Governors, as bearing a responsible list of signatures. In order to enable the dissident members to voice and discuss their complaints – and because it has often been declared that they do not have enough say in the affairs of the Institute – a series of open meetings dealing with different aspects of its work was arranged at the NFT. These were to begin with an introductory talk by the head of the department involved, and then to be thrown open for arguments and questions. However, they were so poorly attended that they had to be accounted a failure. "The only real discussion," says Stanley Reed, "was on the editorial policy of *Sight and Sound*, an issue which was to recur. On matters more relevant to the points brought out in the letter people were surprisingly uninterested, and ignored an opportunity for the 'dialogue' they had been asking for." In the circumstances it seems natural that the BFI should conclude that the criticisms were not so widely or deeply felt as had appeared from the open letter.

The organisation continues to be plagued by the diffusion of its offices, with its consequent inconvenience for officers and staff. The acquisition of Royalty House, only a few yards from 81 Dean Street, in 1969, eased the situation, and a number of scattered rooms in Old Compton Street and elsewhere have been centralised. Even so, at the end of 1970 the BFI's affairs were spread over seven buildings: the main administrative offices in 81 Dean Street and Royalty House, with an offshoot in the original 4 Great Russell Street, the National Film Theatre on South Bank, the Film Production Board's premises in Lower Marsh, near Waterloo Station, and the two Archive centres at Aston Clinton, Bucks, and Berkhamstead, Herts.

In its periodical review, *Outlook, 1965,* the BFI somewhat gloomily summarised and stressed its financial needs. "It was set up in 1933 with the idea that it would 'enjoy sufficient funds and independence of action to enable it to promote the various uses of the film as a contribution to national well-being.' The 'sufficient funds' amounted, at the outset, to an annual grant of less than £9,000 a year from the Cinematograph Fund. . . . Since [1948 and the Radcliffe Committee] the Institute has advanced rapidly and effectively on all fronts. . . . Yet [it] remains conscious that the broad terms of reference laid down for it by the Government have often had to be too narrowly interpreted, because of the constant pressure to make ends meet financially."

In 1966–67 the grant totalled £230,000 – a respectable sum but not – as *Outlook* pointed out – over generous when compared with Covent Garden's million. Earnings were estimated about the same as the previous year. A small but welcome addition was brought in by the success of Peter Watkins' *The War Game* (1967). The film was originally made for the BBC, but they had decided that its treatment and subject matter (a realistic representation of the effects of nuclear bombardment) might prove too alarming for the viewer vulnerably isolated in his own home, and decided not to televise it. Watkins was already known to the BFI through his other work and Stanley Reed approached Kenneth Adam, Director of BBC TV and also at that time an Institute governor,

The headquarters of the British Film Institute, 81 Dean Street, W1

The first home of the BFI,
Great Russell Street, WCI

Interior of the Telekinema,
South Bank – first home of
the National Film Theatre

to negotiate for the distribution rights of *The War Game*. It was given a number of special screenings at the NFT and afterwards achieved wide distribution throughout the world. At the end of 1970 it was still bringing the BFI an income.

In the last weeks of 1970, as this book was nearing completion, a manifesto was issued by a group of members who had formed themselves into an 'Action Group', in which they stated a number of grievances. Extracts from this manifesto were published, and enlarged upon, in an issue of the magazine *Time Out*, and replied to by various members of the Institute in the following number. In the opinion of the Action Committee the Governors were "(mostly would-be and not-quite) moguls and tycoons, whose main interest is money, with a fringe of peers of the realm, wheeler-dealers and culture heroes." (The Board at the end of 1970 consisted of Sir William Coldstream, Chairman, Paul Adorian, Edgar Anstey, Jocelyn Baines, Sir Michael Balcon, Professor Asa Briggs, Kevin Brownlow, R. S. Camplin, J. S. Christie, John H. Davis, Carl Foreman, Mrs Helen Forman, G. M. Hoellering, Dr D. L. Kerr and Lord Lloyd of Hampstead.) The Action Committee complained, *inter alia*, that Institute funds were dissipated on regional film theatres, and wanted no more opened; that BFI publications tried to monopolise the market; that the Production Board saw itself as a Hollywood giant, and should not produce feature films; that the Archive stored films instead of showing them, and did not accept all the films it was offered – and did not seek vigorously enough for a statutory deposit ruling. A resolution was to be put forward at the annual general meeting to remove from office each of the fifteen governors. The signatories to the Manifesto were Ian Cameron, Steve Dwoskin, Simon Field, Mark Forstater, Nick Garnham, Jon Halliday, Simon Hartog, Phil Hardy, Maurice Hatton, Claire Johnston, Geoffrey Nowell Smith, Victor Perkins, Peter Sainsbury and Peter Wollen.

The A.G.M., a livelier function than usual and, exceptionally but not unexpectedly, crammed to the roof, took place on 14th December under imminent threat of being plunged into actual as well as metaphorical darkness by electricity cuts. In reply to the proposal to oust the Governors, Sir William Coldstream read the following statement:

D

"The British Film Institute is a public body, in fact a charity, and it is dependent on an annual grant from the Department of Education and Science. The Minister has the sole power to appoint the Governors. The Governors, themselves, receive no payment for their work and accept office because they believe in the importance of the Film and the need for a Film Institute.

"The Institute is here to serve the general public; it is not a club. This does not mean that the Governors are not concerned with the members' views, but it does mean that the Governors have a duty beyond the membership to the whole public.

"At the present time the Institute has nearly 15,000 full members and 65,000* associate members. Out of this membership fifteen have come together under the title of an "Action Committee". Their declared aim is to remove from office all the Governors, hence the resolutions before you today.

"The Governors are people with considerable experience in the arts, films, education and business. They are people who either make films or go to films and they all care about films. Over the past six years, the period substantially covered by your present Governors, much has been achieved. However, when I took over as Chairman in 1964 we were faced with many problems. The Archive had a very large number of films which were in danger of disintegrating and needed copying. It was growing and urgently needed new storage accommodation. We had neither the facilities not the money for such a development. The Experimental Film Fund was exhausted – the Institute had no money to give young film-makers. The National Film Theatre was in trouble. It had moved to make room for a major expansion but, as you know, this scheme collapsed through no fault of the Institute and we returned to our old home on the South Bank. This abortive move cost us much goodwill and many members. All the central services of the Institute were under pressure, not least the Information Department, where they were attempting to cope with a demand far in excess of their resources. There was also much criticism of the Institute confining its activities to London. In addition the Institute was in financial difficulties. The Government grant was going up, but at a rate which barely took account of rising costs

* This figure includes Regional members, I.B.

and our revenue from other sources was under £100,000. It is against this background that I should like to remind you of a few of the achievements of your Governors.

1. We have secured a permanent home for the Archive – an Archive which is recognised as amongst the best in the world – and six acres of land is available for further expansion. They should more than satisfy our needs for many years ahead. We have rehoused and extended the Information Department and Library and established a separate reading room for students.

2. We have opened a second theatre within the National Film Theatre complex. Before the end of the financial year a restaurant and a new club room will also be opened. We have already instituted an 'Open Night' when new young film-makers can show examples of their work at the NFT.

3. We have built up the John Player series of lectures, at no cost to the Institute, which has brought scores of film-makers and actors on to the stage of the National Film Theatre.

4. We have pressed for statutory deposit for the Archive and thanks to Dr David Kerr, one of our Governors, this matter has been sympathetically debated in both Houses of Parliament.

5. We have started the Production Board. In doing this we have for the first time secured Government support in making money from our grant available to help young film-makers. Since 1966 when experimental production was restarted, over sixty films have been made and eight more are now in production.

6. We have set up thirty-six regional film theatres within the past three years. These have been arranged in close co-operation with local film societies and local authorities. If proof is needed of the welcome these have received from Local Authorities, I think it is enough to say that the Local Authorities have contributed nearly six pounds to the capital costs for every one pound put up by the Institute.

"In essence, the policy of establishing regional theatres is to show film programmes which would otherwise not be available, to the maximum number of people. This means the whole of the country and not merely London and a few big cities. This was the corner-stone of our regional policy.

"Lastly, we have pressed for a National Film School and we are delighted that the plans are now well advanced and the school is expected to open in September 1971. Much of the credit for this should go to one of the Governors, Lord Lloyd, who has been largely responsible for this development.

"This brief resumé illustrates some of the achievements of the British Film Institute and the reasons why it has won international regard.

"I do not want, however, to give the impression that we are satisfied with things as they are. Or course we are not. There is much more we want to do. In particular, we have in mind the need to provide more prints for the Archive so that its films may be made more accessible.

"I have purposely not mentioned money, although it is relevant that the Governors have secured an increase of no less then 400 per cent over these six years, bringing the Government grant to £500,000. With a larger budget, we could obviously have achieved more. As I have said, we are dependent on a Government grant and I am concerned lest the Government should see any cause to cut back their support of our activities.

"Your Governors are always willing and ready to discuss ways of improving the workings of the Institute with all interested parties. I am told that these resolutions to remove the Governors from office are being put forward to promote discussion and ensure that the views of these fifteen members are heard by the Institute's Governors and staff. This would, in my opinion, be a valid argument if this Action Committee had already made an attempt to present their views to the Governors. This is not the case, since at no time has the Action Committee made any representation to me personally, or my colleagues, for a meeting.

"I ask those members who, I am sure, have the interests of the Film and this Institute at heart; do they seriously want their resolutions passed? Because if they are passed a vacuum will be created – a vacuum which they cannot themselves fill since members can remove Governors from office but cannot elect replacements. This is the prerogative of the Minister. I take this opportunity of assuring the members of the Action Committee that I am prepared to arrange an early and mutually convenient date when their proposals can be discussed.

"I ask them at this hour to withdraw their resolutions which, if passed, can only harm the Institute. If they are not prepared to withdraw, I urge all members to reject the resolutions and support the Governors."

The Action Committee generously made it clear that their resolutions (read out singly for each governor) was in no way a personal vendetta against any of them, but claimed that this was the only way in which the points it wished to raise could be brought into open discussion, and after a lengthy debate, conducted at times with rather more vigour than clarity, the proposal for the removal of each and all of the Governors was put to the vote, and defeated by 187 votes to 90. At the insistence of three of the Action Committee members, a postal vote was forced upon the Institute, involving a cost of over £1,000 – money which, it might be thought, could have been spent to better purpose. Of the 4,425 members who returned voting forms, 225 voted for the removal of all the Governors, 3,852 voted for their retention. The remaining 348 mixed their votes, voting for or against the retention of individual Governors. An analysis of the total number of votes cast showed that approximately 8 per cent were in favour of removing Governors, and 92 per cent wished to retain them. According to the Action Committee the result was a foregone conclusion since only one side of the argument was sent out to members with the voting form. In their turn the Institute pointed out that the Action Committee, like everyone else, was at perfect liberty to approach BFI members – a list of whom is available, under the Companies Act (which the Action Committee had invoked), upon payment of a fee.

Perhaps the most constructive suggestion that came out of the whole protest was a plea at the AGM from Sir Arthur Elton for better communication on its activities and intentions – possibly in the form of a regular newsletter or bulletin – between the BFI and its members.

For the financial year 1969–70 the Institute achieved a surplus of £2,620 after making provision for the operating deficits of the three directly run Film Theatres at Brighton, Tyneside and the London NFT. This compared favourably with a deficit the previous year of £37,060. A general grant of £409,113 was received from the Department of Education and Science, together with two special grants – of £50,000 and £58,521 – the latter for capital expenditure on regional projects. Public support for the Institute was indicated by the response to an appeal for funds launched in September 1969: by the end of March 1970 subscriptions from members and the public had totalled £5,249 and deeds of covenant had been taken out with a grossed-up value of £11,881. The six years since Sir William Coldstream took over as Chairman and Stanley Reed as Director saw the total grant raised from £147,000 to over £500,000, and the Institute's earnings from £95,000 to £238,000.*

Membership figures towards the end of 1970 stood at 14,298 full, and 18,818 associate. The associate figures at present fluctuate considerably, owing mainly to increases in subscription. Full membership shows on balance a small but steady increase: this includes the right to purchase three guest tickets at the NFT, receipt of the programme booklet and *Sight and Sound* free, the *Monthly Film Bulletin* at a reduced rate, and use of the Information Department, Book and Stills Libraries and film hire service.

In 1934 the BFI staff numbered about a dozen – today it is somewhere in the region of 230, and this is still inadequate to cope with the volume of work. It is probably fair to state here that among similar bodies the Institute, though not blameless, is one of the least addicted to wastage of its resources. And ultimately it all depends on these. "Everything we plan or hope to accomplish," says Stanley Reed, "is restricted by lack of funds: everything that we have accomplished has been in spite of this."

In any consideration of what the BFI has or has not achieved, or whether it does or does not fall short of some particular objective, this sordid and material fact should be borne in mind.

* In 1971 the Institute received its largest grant, £750,000, but of this, £50,000 was to be regarded as a bonus that might not be renewed.

2

Preservation

1. The National Film Archive

History

"A kind of National Gallery should be started for the collection of films of all public events including last year's Jubilee." This admirable suggestion appeared in a publication entitled *The Magic Lantern*. The year – 1899. Unfortunately, it was over thirty years before any steps were taken towards acting on it, by which time an incalculable amount of invaluable historical material had been irrevocably lost, and a unique opportunity of studying the emergence of an art form from its very beginnings had gone for ever.

When the BFI was established in 1933 one of the objects set before it was the setting up and maintenance of a "national repository of films of permanent value". Even then the wheels were very slow in starting to turn. A National Film Library was proposed in September 1934, but was not formally constituted until May 1935, and then only as a part-time activity of one member of the Institute's very small staff. That member was Ernest Lindgren, who has been Curator of what is now known as the National Film Archive for the whole of its thirty-five years. While he was at London University as a student, Ernest Lindgren had been a frequent visitor to the specialised cinemas in the West End, finding there a type of film excitingly different from the family houses he had so far known, and on discovering by chance a copy of a shilling booklet in the library entitled *The Film in National Life*, became fired with the realisation of the enormous potentialities of the medium. He applied for a job advertised by the British Film Institute, and failed to get it. "But it happened that, by a very rare chance, the Institute actually had a little money to spare," he recalls, "so they created a new post of Information

Officer and asked me if I would like to take it on. I was so anxious to join that I'd have agreed to anything – so they showed me a small pile of books in a corner and said: that's our reference library, will you organise it?"

Being, as he describes himself, a librarian *manqué*, he set to work happily to catalogue the meagre stock of volumes on a system he invented himself, but soon realised that however well this might work for him, it was less comprehensible to others. This proved a significant discovery, for it led him henceforth to eschew all such private systems and to turn instead for the cataloguing, not only of the Information and Book Library but later also the Archive's film collection, to standard procedures of the library world, and to employ qualified librarians on the Archive staff. In particular, as the result of a fruitful contact with Dr Bradley of the Science Museum Library, it led him to adopt the Universal Decimal Classification for which Dr Bradley was the leading pioneer in this country.

After a short time the subject of a film library was broached and he was asked if he would like to prepare a plan: he became so enthusiastic about the idea that when it was finally decided to go ahead the scheme was put into his hands. There was no money, no films, and no equipment. Money, as always, was the laggard, though donations were received from, among others, H. G. Wells and David Low, the cartoonist. Bernard Shaw made out a bankers order for £10 per annum which continued until his death – it is doubtful whether the amount caused him undue privation. "It was born in poverty," says Lindgren, "and reared in poverty, and is still very far short of the financial resources it needs to perform its task with complete efficiency."

Copies of films, however, did start to trickle in, the largest single batch in these early days coming from Harry Price. R. S. Lambert, as we have seen, was a close friend of Price, and persuaded him to present the Library with his valuable private collection of pre-1914 films, which he did, together with £100 in cash. As a result of this generous gift, and on account of his interest in the work of the Institute as a whole, Price was elected first Chairman of the National Film Library.

With no equipment, projectors, viewing tables or moviolas,

Lindgren, still the one and only member of the staff, worked in primitive conditions proper to a pioneer, identifying for instance an early acquisition as Edwin Porter's *Great Train Robbery* by holding the first few feet up to the window and comparing the frames of the films with an illustration in Benjamin Hampton's *History of the Movies*. The *Great Train Robbery*, together with early films of the Lumière brothers, Charles Chaplin and John Bunny, as well as D. W. Griffith's *Birth of a Nation*, was included in the first public performance given by the Archive at the Polytechnic Cinema, London, on 21st February 1936, to commemorate the fortieth anniversary of the first public film performance in Britain (likewise given at the Polytechnic by the Lumière brothers in 1896); the Rt. Hon. Sir Herbert Samuel, later Lord Samuel, was the guest of honour.

Slowly equipment, more films – and even a little money – began to come in, and soon the space available at Great Russell Street, where the Institute's offices were situated at the time, proved inadequate for their storage. A number of vaults were rented in Denmark Street, Soho, which became the Archive's first home of its own. A valuable acquisition in 1938 was a batch of some 200 films handed over for preservation by the Stoll Company when they gave up their Cricklewood studios. Titles included the 1921 version of *Kipps*, starring George K. Arthur (who later sprang to fame in Josef von Sternberg's first film, *The Salvation Hunters*); *The Rocks of Valpré*, and early Ivor Novello melodrama; the first English feature film in colour, *The Glorious Adventure*, starring Lady Diana Manners and the Great Fire of London; D. W. Griffiths's *Hearts of the World;* and a number of short Sherlock Holmes adventures with Eille Norwood, arguably the best Sherlock of them all. In the same year C. B. Cochran placed the Palace Theatre at the Library's disposal for a special show which consisted of *Kipps*, Anthony Asquith's *A Cottage on Dartmoor* and excerpts from Hitchcock's *The Lodger* and *Blackmail*. About the same time a non-recurrent grant of £3,000 was received from the Cinematograph Fund, and the first Selection Committee was appointed under A. C. Cameron, one of the Institute's governors.

By now some 400 films had been acquired, ranging widely

from *The Great Train Robbery* to an esoteric trio entitled $X+X=O$, $X+X=Asin\ Nt$ and *Euclid 132*, and the Library had been divided into two sections, Loan and Preservation. At the start of 1939 it was beginning to be realised that the rented film vaults in Denmark Street were insufficient for a permanent repository such as the National Film Library, and that it would be necessary to seek permanent premises. At first the plan was to engage an architect to design special accommodation, but this had to be abandoned for the usual reason – lack of funds. Eventually all these somewhat leisurely proceedings were interrupted by the outbreak of the Second World War and the Government order for the immediate removal from London of all large stocks of inflammable material, in particular nitrate film. The story of the Film Library's exodus has been briefly told in the first part of this book. Temporary accommodation was found in a stables in the Sussex village of Rudgwick. To have secured even so humble a lodging was something of a triumph, as every film company in town was seeking similar refuge. The next door stable was inhabited by British Movietone News, and just across the farm courtyard Paramount had taken up quarters. Even in such august company, It was obvious that this could be only a temporary resting place, and Ernest Lindgren immediately began an intensive search for more permanent quarters, setting himself limits of more than twenty but less than forty miles from London – in a north-westerly direction. In what can only be regarded as a spirit of optimism in those evacuation days he travelled from place to place, finishing up, empty-handed, in Oxford. Returning somewhat despondently to London, he was glancing through his pile of estate agent forms and suddenly noticed one which mentioned Aston Clinton. Jumping off the train at Aylesbury, he hurried to the agent, went over the property, and shortly afterwards the Institute acquired one-third of an acre, with a new house and outbuildings on three sides – for £950 freehold. With the house as offices and laboratories, and the outbuildings converted into storage vaults, these premises at Aston Clinton served as sole repository for the Library for over twenty years.

Apart from this notable achievement, the war period was a period of frustration for the National Film Library as it was for most worth-while activities, though the collection was increased whenever opportunity offered. In 1941 the Ministry of Information for instance decided to present copies of all its films for preservation by the Library: how much chaff-sifting this entailed is not recorded. The Lending Section Catalogue published at the end of the war (no complete catalogue was issued between 1938 and 1951) listed some 100 titles, dating from 1895 to 1943, mainly shorts or extracts, and mainly from the silent period. Only nine sound features were available, including *Blackmail, The Foreman Went to France, The Blue Angel* and *Kameradschaft.* The score or so of silent features contained a large proportion of German and Russian classics (*Battleship Potemkin, Mother, The General Line, Metropolis, Waxworks, The Last Laugh*), the only British title being *A Cottage on Dartmoor.*

The 1948 the Radcliffe Report commented on the inadequacy of this lending section (an inadequacy due solely to lack of money) and attached the "greatest importance" to its being built up. Noting also that the number of titles in the preservation section stood at around 3,000 and the collection of stills at 25,000, it summed up its conclusions and recommendations that the Institute "should develop the National Film Library to form a comprehensive collection of significant films; develop facilities for individual and group study of films and the showing of special programmes; considerably extend the lending side of its library; reorganise and improve its information section; concentrate its publishing on authoritative work of high standard; stimulate and itself undertake academic research; and develop a regional organisation to extend its influence and services." This was, of course, only setting down on paper what had been the aims of the Library since its inception.

During 1948 the Library compiled and issued a number of *Critic and Film* shorts in which well-known critics discussed sequences from films (e.g. Jympson Harmon on *Great Expectations* and Dilys Powell on *The Overlanders*) treating the subjects in ways which assumed varying degrees of knowledge in the viewer. Unfortunately this interesting series was short-lived. Two years later steps were taken to bring the collection further into public notice by inaugurating a repertory season of films to illustrate the historical progress of the cinema. Programmes were arranged from the preservation section by Ernest Lindgren. The first season, held at the Institut Français in South Kensington, included Hitchcock's *The Lodger*, Griffiths' *Hearts of the World*, Pabst's *L'Atlantide*, Dovzhenko's *Earth*, Harold Lloyd's *Safety Last* and Clair's *The Italian Straw Hat*. Similar programmes were given later on two evenings a week in the small viewing theatre at Great Russell Street. In these performances could be seen the beginnings of a national film theatre.

In 1955 the Library's title was changed to the National Film Archive, to underline the importance of its preservation function; 'library', in the film industry, usually means 'distribution library', and was open to misunderstanding. Seven years earlier, in an article in *Penguin Film Review No. 5*, Lindgren had expressed his dislike of the word 'archive', with its intimations of grim stone archways leading to dank dungeons and catacombs. "It rings," he wrote then, "with a deathly sound in the world of the cinema, which is so young, vital and dynamic." Film Museum, however, would be even worse, and it is difficult to think of a suitable alternative. "There is no reason," Lindgren pointed out, "why a film archive should be a mausoleum." With its change of title, the National Film Archive also achieved a greater amount of independence as a self-managing body within the Institute.

Once again, as storage and technical requirements grew, it became increasingly clear that present premises would be insufficient for the Archive's needs. In 1960 consideration began to be given to the problem of finding an additional site – and the money to pay for it. With the encouragement of the Treasury, the Institute's Governors enlisted the aid of the Ministry of Public Building and Works in a search for premises within reasonable distance of Aston Clinton. The wheels of Government following their usual divine precept of grinding exceeding slow, it took several years for anything much to happen, but eventually, and with the vigorous help once again of Miss Jennie Lee, a site in Berkhamsted was bought with a grant of £28,000 from the Department of Education and Science, and a further grant of £36,000 was made for the erection of additional buildings, including modern storage vaults. The generosity of these grants has to be measured against the Berlin Film Archive's receipt for building accommodation in the same year of £750,000. Nevertheless, with this money the Archive was able to purchase a 5½-acre estate, with a large and attractive building dating in part from Tudor times, Kingshill House in pleasant Green Belt surroundings and at a convenient distance from Aston Clinton. The new premises were officially opened by Mrs Gwyneth Dunwoody, Parliamentary Secretary to the Board of Trade, in May 1968. When fully developed it is hoped that Kingshill, together with Aston Clinton, will prove adequate to the needs of the National Film Archive for a great many years to come.

Selection and acquisition

The first Selection Committee was set up in 1938 for the purpose of advising on films of "permanent importance" to be preserved in the Library. Today the Archive employs three acquisition officers, responsible for keeping themselves informed not only of films but also of television programmes, and for trying to persuade the owners to deposit copies. *"In selection, they depend on the help of four advisory committees. A General Selection Committee, composed mainly of film critics, representing a wide range of viewpoint, advises on feature films, and films as art and entertainment. For non-fiction films, assistance is given by a History Selection Committee composed of historians and subject experts, and a Science Selection Committee of scientists and people with an interest in scientific or technical films, many of them members or officers of the British Industrial and Scientific Film Association. For television, [the Archive has] the assistance of a Television Advisory Committee, composed mainly of people working in BBC television or in Independent television, and a number of television critics." The acquisition officers make a first choice, and this list is submitted to further scrutiny until a final selection can be made up of suggestions for the committees to consider. The latter are also supplied with copies of the *Monthly*

* Unless otherwise indicated, quotations in this section are from articles by Ernest Lindgren and Clyde Jeavons in the *Journal of the Society of Film and Television Arts*, Spring 1970.

Film Bulletin and the *British National Film Catalogue* to see what has been omitted. Much the same method is applied to television, but here there is the additional problem that the programmes, once transmitted, may not be seen again. The committees then consider each film on the list in turn, discuss its archival merits, and try to arrive at a decision as to whether the Archive should be recommended to acquire it, or whether to let it go. Since selection is basically imperfect, and since a film wrongly acquired can always at some future time be jettisoned, whereas a film wrongly rejected may be lost for ever, the decision need not be unanimous, nor even necessarily a majority one: a minority recommendation will sometimes be accepted. "The basic criterion is a very simple one. Anyone assessing a film for preservation in the Archive is asked to view it with one question constantly in the forefront of his mind, from sequence to sequence, from shot to shot: namely: Is there any conceivable reason of form or content, or of external association of any kind, why the loss of this film, fifty years hence or five hundred years hence, would be regretted? If the answer is 'yes', then this may be a justification for keeping it: if it is an emphatic 'Yes', then it certainly will be so."

Selection committees are required to agree on a reason, however brief, for each selection. This is recorded in the minutes and then transferred to the catalogue entries. The purpose of this is not to provide embryonic programme notes, but to compel selectors to justify their choice, to provide a basis for discussion if opinions differ, and a basis of agreement which a majority, or a sufficient number, of committee members feel able to support.

A question often asked is whether there is any particular line laid down for selection, any particular title or titles which the Archive is especially proud to have acquired. The answer, in each case, is 'no'. The range is the important consideration, and it is impossible to single out any one film, period or type. Nor is it by any means certain that the 'best film' of its day will be the most interesting to preserve for the future. Indeed a cheap, hastily concocted 'B' picture may well be more representative of its period, or even more significant of the contemporary cinema, than a costly prestige production. Lindgren makes another point: "A film can be a great popular success: look at it ten or twenty years later, and you may think, 'What rubbish!' But keep it *another* ten or twenty years and you begin to realise why it was so popular at the particular moment of its release. As in the case of feminine fashion, it will begin to acquire a new charm or interest of its own."

Every film shown in this country, whatever its source, is considered to come within the Archive's province. The world's movie cameras never stop churning, and it is obviously neither possible nor desirable to keep every film made, even were the selectors granted foreknowledge of what would appear of interest in twenty years time. "In 1969 over 450 foreign and ninety British feature films were shown for the first time in Britain, apart from hundreds of documentaries, cartoons and industrial shorts, and excluding altogether the television programmes. Of all these, the Selection Committees listed some ninety films as worthy of preservation, ranging from *Oedipus* to *The Night They Raided Minsky's*.* Selection is inevitable. It can only be made, as far as possible, representative, and even this involves a certain kind of censorship. It is not, of course, a problem confined to the film. Masterpieces may survive in any art, but who can tell how many literary works of at least reasonable merit have been pulped and lost, how many paintings worth preservation have rotted away in cellars? Film's especial problem – at least in reference to early years – is that its very substance, unlike paper, paint or canvas, so soon disintegrates.

Thirty years ago, in 1940, a list was published by the Selection Committee of the twelve stars whose films were considered most worth keeping. They were: Theda Bara, Charlie Chaplin, Douglas Fairbanks (snr), Greta Garbo, Mary Pickford, Rudolph Valentino, Fred Astaire, Spencer Tracy, Tom Mix, Harold Lloyd, Marie Dressler, and Shirley Temple. (No Buster Keaton, no W. C. Fields, no Lillian Gish, even though the list was apparently limited to America.)

Film selection is only the beginning, and the easier part, of the job. Having chosen what it wants, the Archive now has to get hold of them. As Clyde Jeavons, head of the Acquisition Depart-

* David Gordon on *Why the National Film Archive?* – Cinema City Catalogue, 1970.

ment, says: "There is no statutory deposit of films in the United Kingdom, comparable to the statutory deposit of books in the library of the British Museum, and the Archive is almost totally dependent for the growth of its collection on voluntary gifts from the film industry; the money it has to buy films is negligible. . . .

"Co-operation from film companies is sporadic and inconsistent, and this does much to destroy the balance of representation which the Archive's selection committees spend so much time and care in trying to achieve. Some companies blankly refuse to give copies of their films to the Archive, or keep the Archive waiting for many years, creating the uncertainty of whether the films will eventually be received or not; others give inconsistent help, co-operating at some periods and not at others, or giving some films and withholding others. Some small companies, or individual film-makers, especially of documentary or short films, often have no choice but to refuse the Archive's request because they have no copy which they can spare and can certainly not afford to make one specially. Similarly, distributors of continental and foreign language films import very few copies and as these are for specialised exhibition over a long period, the handful which are eventually offered to the Archive are often so worn as to make the offer, and its acceptance, pointless."

Nor does this attitude of reserve on the part of the industry apply only to the actual supply of copies. In 1968, as reported in the BFI *Outlook* for the year, the Gulbenkian Foundation promised £7,500 towards the making of Archive show prints for use in education and film theatres. The money was to be spent either on making duplicate copies of master material already held in the Archive, or on obtaining material from other sources that could be placed in the Archive's custody. The relevant departments of the Institute agreed on a list of priorities and a number of companies were asked to make prints, and to allow them to be shown, subject to their specific authority. With a very few exceptions, the response was negative. Either the company insisted on holding the prints (which was outside the terms of the Gulbenkian offer), or they refused altogether for fear of prejudicing commercial exploitation. Another difficulty against which the NFA has to contend – and one which sometimes causes indignant outcries

National Film Archive vaults at Aston Clinton

National Film Archive, Kingshill House, Berkhamsted, house and film storage block

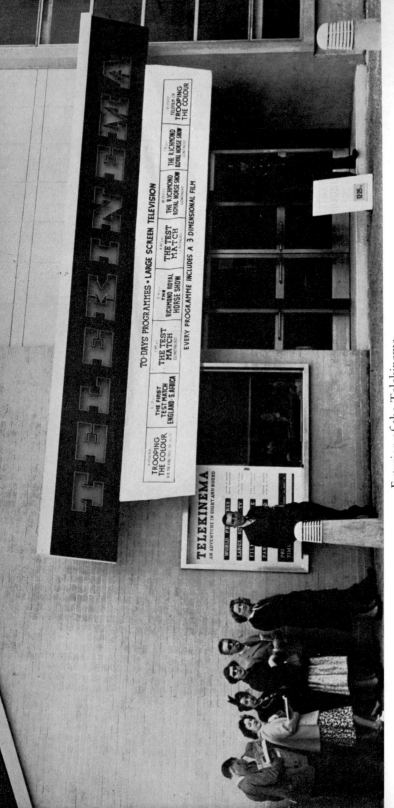

Exterior of the Telekinema

when Archive films are shown at the National Film Theatre – is the condition of the prints supplied. "Worn prints," says Jeavons, "are the norm and are accepted *faute de mieux*, even though many are used projection copies which would otherwise be destroyed. In isolated cases – mainly those where printing demands on a film have declined or ceased altogether, or where obsolete nitrate stock is involved – master material of some kind, negative or fine grain positive, is given to the Archive; occasionally, too, documentary or independent film-makers deem it an honour to have their work picked out for posterity, and gladly donate master material or a new print. But these instances are rare."

In the case of television material the position is even more precarious. The BBC, for instance, generally possesses only one copy of a film, which it needs for its own library. Since 1969 ITV programmes are copied under terms of an annual grant (of £10,000) from the ITCA, so that here the position is easier.

The case for a statutory deposit is a strong one. At present the Archive receives on average only some 25 per cent of the films *selected* – the largest proportion being British with nearly 50 per cent and American under 33 per cent. As can be seen, this is a meagre percentage indeed, and would thin the bookshelves to skeletal conditions if applied to the British Museum library. Yet the average routine second-feature picture is at least equally worth preserving as the average routine second-rate novel.

Preservation

Having selected and, with much effort and luck, acquired a copy, the next task is to preserve it. Film stock, even today, is a fragile commodity – in the years before 1952 it was much more so.

*"The preservation process consists in acquiring a master preservation copy in the best possible condition (ideally, either the original negative or a perfectly processed new fine-grain duplicating print for black-and-white film, or for colour a set of black-and-white separations, taken as a first copy from the original

---

* Unless otherwise indicated, all quotations in this section are from an article by Harold G. Brown, Film Preservation Officer of the Archive, in the *Journal of the Society of Film and Television Arts*, Spring 1970.

E

negative), keeping it under recommended and constant conditions of temperature and humidity, examining it or testing it at necessary intervals, and otherwise protecting it from all avoidable handling or wear. If a film is kept in this way, its photographic emulsion (except for the fading of colour dyes) will last indefinitely. The base or support, however, will not, and it is this which lies at the heart of most of the preservation problems and procedures."

The problem is divided into two main parts: movies made before, and those made after, 1952. Until that year every standard film was made on nitrate stock.

"This material, apart from its inflammability, is an inherently unstable chemical compound which, as soon as it is manufactured, begins to decompose; slowly at first but gradually accelerating. The gaseous products of decomposition affect the image layer of the film, causing fading of the image and effecting changes which lead it readily to absorb atmospheric moisture and become sticky. At this stage the film is quite useless. Unfortunately there is no change in the film visibly apparent until the image is damaged, and although decomposition proceeds slowly for many years, the film may pass from an apparently perfectly normal, usable condition to complete uselessness within a few months." The decomposition of nitrate film proceeds more slowly if it is kept at a low and constant temperature. When the Aston Clinton property was bought, the outbuildings (stables or cattlesheds) were converted, and for the first time vaults were constructed *inside* another building, as a sort of inner shell. This made control of temperature a simpler matter because of the envelope of air surrounding the vaults. In addition, the outer walls of the buildings were painted white to modify the heat of the sun in summer. Such storage, however, is expensive, cumbersome, and in the end ineffective because, whatever the conditions, nitrate film will eventually decompose. A technical committee of outside experts from the Kodak and Ilford Companies and from Government laboratories etc., was called in and advised that, rather than go in for the heavy expense of full air-conditioning, any money should be spent on regular testing, *reasonably* good storage conditions, and the making of copies on acetate stock as soon as the film showed the first signs of instability.

To this end, as soon as each film is received by the Archive – or as soon as possible – it is tested, and the test repeated at periodic intervals. The test involves "punching out a disc of film ¼ inch in diameter. The discs punched out are placed each in a small test tube and the open end plugged with a glass stopper around which is an indicator paper of Alizarin Red. The samples are heated to 134 degrees centigrade in air baths. The heat accelerates the de-composition of the sample which releases acid vapours, the presence of which is revealed by bleaching of the indicator paper. The time at which this occurs is recorded and affords an indication of a certain minimum remaining life."

The Archive has been copying films since 1942, but it is a formidably expensive process. To copy at once all the films at present stored would cost £1½ million. Even under good condi-tions nitrate film cannot be expected to have a usable life of more than some forty years. Thus an annual copying programme which would enable the total holding to be completed within that period would cost about £30,000 p.a. Until recently only about £3,000 to £4,000 p.a. was available, so that it was obvious that in time the necessary annual sum would rise astronomically. (There is also, of course, in these inflationary days, the constantly increasing actual cost of the work to consider). However, in 1970, for the first time, a sum of £37,750 has been earmarked by the Depart-ment of Education and Science for this purpose, and this, as at present arranged, will be paid each year until the whole nitrate collection has been preserved.

Since 1952 the preservation position has been much eased because of the almost universal use of cellulose-tri-acetate safety film. This is reasonably stable, with a life measured in centuries rather than decades, and is also non-inflammable. With the purchase of Kingshill, Berkhamsted, the position improved still further. Apart from very much increased storage space (important not only from the simple question of room, but also because it is inadvisable to keep nitrate and post-1952 acetate films together as the acid fumes from the former can affect the condition of the latter), one annex has been specially insulated and air-conditioned to maintain a deep-freeze atmosphere for colour films. Colour is, of course, almost as old as the movies themselves, but it is only comparatively recently – with the arrival of colour television and the relentless demands of that insatiable Moloch – that its almost universal employment was adopted. Its preservation set a new problem almost as soon as the arrival of acetate film had partially solved the old one. "Whereas the image on a black and white film, if properly fixed and adequately washed, enjoys a very high degree of permanency," says Harold Brown, "this is not true of colour film. The picture on colour film consists, not of silver as for a black and white film, but of dye; and dyes are notoriously subject to change and fade. This is particularly true of the dyes which have to be used to obtain a colour photograph. These must necessarily fulfil so many other requirements that the possible substances are limited; and permanency is not as good as one would like. Indeed, in the case of some materials, colours can change significantly within a few years and we must be prepared at least for difficulties in copying from any of them after twenty-five years." Hence the building of the experimental deep-freeze store at Kingshill, capable of being maintained at any temperature down to minus 18 degrees centigrade, which Kodak scientists suggested on theoretical grounds as being an ideal at which to aim. Recent laboratory research, however, suggests that there may be little to be gained by going below minus 5 degrees centigrade. The vault is capable of holding 2,700 large reels, the equivalent of some 250 feature films. Low humidity is also important, and special precautions have to be taken to prevent moisture forming when the film is taken from store. But, as Brown points out, "just as the best possible storage conditions will not keep nitrate indefinitely, so even low temperatures will not indefinitely prevent the dyes of colour film from change of hue and fading. The alternative is to keep colour film subjects in the form of a set of three 'separation' films, each of which contains in black and white terms the record of one of the primary colours. These separations can be stored as black and white film and enjoy as long a life. From these it is posible at any future time to produce colour copies. As always, there is a price to pay: they are expensive to make and the process demands a very high standard of mechanical precision." In addition, of course, it would entail holding a separate sound track and would require more than three times the storage space.

Finally there is a further threat to both nitrate and acetate film, to both colour and black and white. This is the possibility of an excessive residue of hypo, the fixing salt, remaining in the film on account of inadequate final washing. To avert this, another test is carried out on newly processed film which, like the nitrate stability test, requires only the punching of a tiny portion. If there is a positive reaction the film is re-washed before storage. All such tests and procedures have been adopted with the guidance and advice of the Archive's Technical Committee, currently under the chairmanship of Bernard Happé, Technical Manager of Technicolor Ltd. The members of the committee, all recognised experts in their fields, give their services free.

Cataloguing

The film has been viewed, considered, selected, acquired, and put into preservation. It now has to be made 'findable' among its 18,000 companions. The present Chief Cataloguer of the Archive, Roger Holman, points out the differences between cataloguing a book and a film: *"In comparison to cataloguing films, the cataloguing of books is relatively easy; necessary information is contained on the title page, that is title, publisher, date (it is now possible to buy sets of printed catalogue cards to file), and although the objective in book cataloguing is identical, not a great deal of time is wasted if by chance an inquirer is given the wrong book. He can simply glance through the table of contents or index and in a few minutes examine half-a-dozen books and return them to the shelf without creating work for the library staff.

"None of this applies when considering a film library and the demands made upon it. Physically each title consists of one or more rolls of celluloid stored in tins which are labelled with the title and the vault location number only. The film itself has no title page, index or table of contents, and its content can only be known after it has been viewed from beginning to end. This examination may take an hour or longer should the inquirer wish

* Unless otherwise indicated, all quotations in this section are taken from an article by Roger Holman in the *Journal of the Society of Film and Television Arts*, Spring 1970.

to gain an overall impression of the film and then possibly re-check individual reels. Should the suggested film be unsatisfactory, an hour of the inquirer's time has been wasted, but much more than one hour of the inquirer's time when we consider the process that precedes this hour's viewing. Each film must be physically handled by Archive staff several times for each viewing: to begin with the film must be removed from the storage vault to the film examination room where it is checked and possibly rewound. The film is then transported by van to the location of the viewing, where it comes under the control of the technical assistant, who is responsible for the viewing. . . . Following viewing, this process is reversed and the film returned to the vaults. Frequent handling of unique preservation material shortens the film's life span and nullifies the care and attention devoted to its preservation. . . . For these reasons it is imperative that the Archive's cataloguing system leads an inquirer not only directly to the required film but, if possible, to the appropriate reel of that film."

The documentation process is divided into three sections:
(a) the Provisional Catalogue, in which every film, whether news-reel, documentary or feature, is immediately listed in a visible strip index, with at this stage inevitably sketchy and often in-accurate details. A number is given, and a certain amount of technical information.
(b) the Permanent Catalogue, which is broken down into six categories – Silent and Sound, each divided into three subsections: Newsfilm, Fiction, and Non-Fiction. Every film is viewed on an editing table and described reel by reel: all details such as cast, production credits, year of release, owner, donor, review refer-ences, date acquired, etc. are entered on a *Main Entry Card*. Three further index cards are then drawn up: A *Subject Index*, for News-films and non-fiction, using the Universal Decimal Classification scheme; a *Biographical Index*, dealing with prominent people in alphabetical order; a *Cast Index* of Fiction films, entering as completely as possible the title of each film in which the actor or actress appears.
(c) the Printed (published) Catalogues, which are virtually printed versions of the Main Entry Cards, often with synopses and descriptions in abbreviated form.

The first complete published catalogue appeared in September 1936, and a second followed in April 1938. The war with its consequent restrictions put an end to complete editions for some years though, as we have seen, catalogues continued to be issued of the Lending Section. Complete catalogues were restarted in 1951, and three volumes have appeared to date:

Part I   – Silent News Films (1895–1933) 1951, with a new updated edition in 1965;

Part II – Silent Non-Fiction Films (1895–1934) 1960;

Part III – Silent Fiction Films (1895–1930) 1966.

A fourth volume will appear shortly, covering Sound Non-Fiction Films (1930–60).

By any standards these published catalogues – the only of their kind in the world – are remarkable achievements, and afford the clearest indication of the great range of the Archive collection, in particular of the silent newsfilms. To read through the three volumes – dealing it should be remembered with the silent cinema alone – is to realise the importance, as social documentation apart from any entertainment or artistic value, of preserving the material they record.

Availability

One complaint above all others is regularly brought against the NFA. "Why is so small a proportion of the films ever available for viewing? What is the point of thousands of reels of uniquely valuable pictures shut up in tin cans in vaults if no-one is ever going to be able to look at them?" 83 per cent of the 18,000 titles cannot be seen, even by the bona fide student. Two main reasons are given for this. The first is technical: it is impossible both to preserve and project a print. The best copy has only a limited projection life. The Kodak Company used to reckon that the films in their library could be projected only about one hundred times. After that, even when used in ideal conditions, they were fit for nothing but to be thrown away. As long ago as 1935 the British Kinematograph Society advised that a preservation copy should *never* be used for projection, but only for making projection copies. All film archives now keep to this rule. The NFA does in fact acquire a certain number of projection copies, partly because many films have survived only in this form – the actual negatives no longer exist. That one copy must be protected – therefore copies must be made. If it is a positive print, then the extra preliminary step is necessary of making a negative from that positive. But there is yet another difficulty: even the negatives used for printing have themselves only a limited life. Used over and over again, they inevitably suffer from handling, from unavoidable wear and tear, from gradual loss of definition.

The second reason concerns copyright. Copyright in a film belongs to the legal owner and is fully protected just as in the case of a book, a play, a piece of music, an invention. Films are received into the Archive on the strict understanding that they are for preservation and, where possible, for private research and study on its premises: for no other use whatever without permission of the owner of the copyright. The question of who *is* the owner is often one of great complexity – and one that often leads to both difficulty and frustration. Cases have been noted in this book where great films have been bought up by studios or interested parties and shelved or even possibly destroyed because a remake was to be put on the market. The right of an owner (as apart from the creator) to dispose of any work of art – or even of entertainment – which can give pleasure and stimulation to hundreds of people, just because he has a financial claim to it, may be morally questioned but cannot, as the law stands at present, be legally put aside.

The NFA depends very largely on voluntary gifts from the film industry, and their essential goodwill and trust would be irrevocably lost were it to play fast and loose in this respect. "We place the greatest emphasis," Ernest Lindgren says, "on our obligation to the people who deposit their films with us. The copyright remains with the owner, who has control over its exhibition, and no copy of a film is ever let out without his permission. No preservation film is projected in any circumstances, even within the Archive's own premises. The film is there as a master copy, and as such it is inviolable. In thirty years no-one has substantiated any complaint of the misuse of a film, and we have never yet lost a single one."

The complaints of inaccessibility are understandable: it does

seem absurd that films should have to be stored away unseen – as absurd as the numerous paintings hidden away in the depths of picture galleries or books collecting dust on forbidden library shelves. The truth is, however, that *anyone* can get *any* film out of the Archive at *any* time for *any* purpose – home screening, televising, global release – provided two conditions are complied with:
(1) that he arranges with the owner or owners of the copyright to provide written permission
(2) that, if a copy has to be made, he provides the money for this. (In the case of an ordinary feature film the cost, if there is no negative in existence, may be anything from £100 to £500 – once a negative has been made, of course, further prints are cheaper.)

The ideal

In the article in *Penguin Film Review* referred to above Ernest Lindgren described his ideal Archive: a large and attractive building in the heart of the metropolis, with an exhibition hall displaying every aspect of film production and film history, stills, set models, posters, apparatus: a 500-seat cinema: a well-equipped book, stills, script, and film music library and reading room, with machines available to provide photographic copies at cost: cubicles where students may examine films on 16mm projectors or on moviolas: a lecture hall: a lending section with 35mm and 16mm prints of all the most important films in the history of the cinema, from Lumière to the latest masterpiece, withdrawn from commercial circulation, in addition to extracts, composite films and instructional films on techniques and production: a fully detailed and constantly up-dated cataloguing department.

It's a long way to Utopia, but, as Lindgren says today: "Over the years we have managed to create a very comprehensive and efficient *design* for an Archive. All the elements are there: it is a simple question, once again, of money."

2. LIBRARY AND INFORMATION

As we have seen, the BFI Library started with a small pile of books in a corner of a room in Great Russell Street which Ernest Lindgren, as the newly created Information Officer, was asked to put in some sort of order. Later the work was taken over by his secretary, Miss Ethel Wakeman. Today, under Miss Brenda Davies, who has been Head of Information for the past fifteen years, it contains over 18,000 volumes – divided into reference and loan sections – about 200 journals regularly received, a card index of some 100,000 entries, innumerable pamphlets and hand-outs, and a comprehensive clippings file from all the British national newspapers, a number of foreign ones, programme notes and similar material.

When Miss Davies came to the Institute (after previously work-ing in the library of the *Daily Telegraph*) the Department was housed in an "evil-smelling basement" in the Shaftesbury Avenue premises, and had a staff of four. It came under the control, for no apparent reason, of the then fairly recent National Film Theatre. Later it was divorced from what appears to have been a somewhat incompatible relationship. In 1954 the O. and M. Department of the Treasury carried out an investigation into the overall admini-stration of the BFI and one of its recommendations, accepted by the Governors, was that the Information Department should be incorporated into the Archive, an arrangement which has worked very satisfactorily ever since. *"Since both the Information and Library Department are within the Archive but have also to serve the British Film Institute and its members, they have a dual function which makes them different in outlook from the average library," says Miss Davies. "As archivists we are building up a collection of books and other material which will be useful to researchers and historians in the distant future and we cannot dispose of our 'surplus' or little-used stock. There is, for instance, very little reader demand for one of our greatest treasures, *Descriptive Zoopraxography or the Science of Animal Locomotion Made Popular* by Eadweard Muybridge, but there can be no doubt of our obligation to hold and preserve books like this which are landmarks in the study of cinema. On the other hand, it is equally our duty to buy and make available to our readers the latest published books on films and film-making."

* Unless otherwise indicated, the quotations in this section are taken from an article by Brenda Davies in the *Journal of the Society of Film and Television Arts*, Spring 1970.

In early days the department was crippled by lack of money, and though things have now improved somewhat, the increasing number of books published on the cinema and allied matters grows faster than the funds allowed for their purchase. In addition to this, the extraordinarily high prices paid for second-hand magazines and books by private collectors at the present time means that the Library is forced into expensive competition for these often indispensable items. Donations and bequests are always welcomed even if the books are already in the stock, as it means not only that more copies can be lent, but also that replacements are available in both sections when the originals become used beyond repair. Windfalls occasionally come along, such as the magnificent *Picture Show* collection, handed over when the magazine became defunct in 1960 and comprising not only a huge pile of periodicals but also a complex and original filing system. This included press notices and cast lists dating from 1917, and individual cards on stars giving not only their films but also personal details such as height, hair colour, eye colour, marriages, age, etc.

The Department is available for use by all members of the BFI and the following annual figures give some indication of the amount of information disseminated by letter, phone or personal calls:

	1961	1968	1969
Letters	1,363	2,046	1,912
External telephone calls	5,663	13,092	16,692
Personal callers	no figures available	3,105	3,623

"The mechanics of running the Library," writes Brenda Davies, "are similar to those of other special libraries. Books are classified under an extension of the Universal Decimal Classification. There are catalogues by author, title and subject, and the collection of over 18,000 volumes is divided into reference and loan sections. Members of the British Film Institute may borrow two books at a time from the loan section, and there is a reading room where books and reference material may be studied."

The numbers using both sections are increasing rapidly with the growth of film study at university levels, and are expected to increase still further when the National Film School is launched. Requests for information range from the simple and expected – such as who directed this or played in that – to the less simple – "Please explain the *exact* workings of the Eady Levy" – and the unexpected – "How can I get my dog on the films?" The most trivial questions are discouraged, and requests for 'fan' information are referred elsewhere. The television companies are frequent seekers after the truth: a package group of films may have been delivered for transmission, with no information provided. The *Radio Times* will telephone to ask the colour of Gary Cooper's eyes – they have a colour illustration to prepare for a forthcoming issue. "We're sometimes stumped," Miss Davies comments, "but we manage to satisfy a good 80 per cent of the queries. It's a help sometimes if we can have some warning of what to expect. We have a large number of foreign visitors, especially from France, where documentation is not easy of access, in particular regarding British and American films. They come flying across the Channel and stand at the counter requiring instant information to fly back with. We're delighted to see them, but it would be a great help if they would let us know in advance when it's something difficult they've come to ask us about."

The 1970–71 budget figures for the department amounted to:

£950 for buying books;
£550 for subscriptions to periodicals;
£550 for binding.

This last is a large item because apart from the normal repair and rebinding of books on loan there is the annual necessity of binding all 200 periodicals in order to preserve them. Wear and tear is a heavy drain on resources, and to this must be added loss by theft and also by deliberate mutilation of magazines while in use in the reading room – a form of filching to which it would seem that film researchers are particularly prone. "People just cut lumps out with razor blades." The American magazine *Films in Review* suffers particularly in this respect, containing as it does very full and well documented life stories of film personalities which are ripped right out by those too lazy to copy the details. Researchers remember with affection the famous 'bags' – hundreds of manilla envelopes each containing press cuttings and other data on one particular film. These will shortly be things of the past as the information is transferred to microseal cards for use on a viewing machine (or, it is hoped, half-a-dozen viewing machines). Apart from the obvious saving in wear and tear of such flimsy material, there will be the added advantage of safeguard against theft. Recently, for instance, when the bag on *Oliver*! was being handed out to an inquirer, it was discovered that it had been stuffed with torn pieces of the *Evening Standard*. Every single cutting had gone. Fortunately in this case Columbia Pictures had filed a complete set of press notices and were able to supply photo-copies, but in many cases (particularly where the notices might have been bad ones) such a loss is irreplaceable. This particularly mean form of stealing is the less excusable since any item required can be photo-copied on the premises for a few pence. In future copies of the microseal cards will also be otainable from a reader-printer, and the valuable originals will be sent for storage at Kingshill, safe from the pilfering of petty predators.

3. THE ARCHIVE STILLS COLLECTION

There are two types of film stills: 'frame stills', which are prints enlarged from an actual frame of the film itself, and 'production stills', which are posed photographs of scenes from the story. The former have the disadvantage of being processed from coarse grain stock (the Archive Stills Department advise that such prints should not exceed 8 inches by 6 inches), but the compensating advantage of a live, 'actual happening' look. The latter are much clearer in texture (and generally reproduce well in 10 inches by 8 inches), but often have an artificial, stilted appearance, particularly when the actors are attempting to 'freeze' violent action. In addition, as many a frustrated filmgoer knows, an enticing still on display outside a cinema may depict a scene which is not to be found on the screen inside.

In the early days of the Archive film stills were merely acquired as part of the general archive materials and a separate department was not set up until about 1948. Since then the collection has grown from a few hundred to its present enormous total of some 700,000 – one of the largest and most comprehensive holdings in the world, and covering the whole history of the cinema.

The great majority of such stills, particularly of recent films, are received from the distributing companies, whose co-operation in general has been generous and wholehearted. The Institute is also the recipient of numerous donations and bequests, many of them of valuable early and rare stills, and also of collections from magazines such as *Picture Show* which have ceased publication. There is also a continual exchange between other Archives. *"Such acquisitions," states Sheila Whitaker, Chief Stills Officer, "presently run at between 15,000 and 20,000 a year. They are captioned with the film title, and each person shown in the still is identified. They are then put in polythene bags and filed under the original title. Two indexes are maintained: one for actors and one for directors and technicians. From then on these stills are available for study and research by students and authors, and where required black and white reproductions are provided."

The growth of demand for copies is indicated by the fact that in 1950 the number supplied was 628, compared with over 13,000 for 1970. There was a sharp intermediate drop (from 10,566 to 8,807) in the years 1968–69 owing to a sudden restriction imposed by certain of the film companies.

Sale of stills is not restricted to members of the Institute, though a higher rate is charged to outsiders. Concerns such as the television companies, requiring a wide range of stills for transmission in various programmes, authors and publishers, form a large part of those requiring copies, but there is also a considerable sale to the private collector and the film 'fan'. Action stills and glamour portraits sell in about equal quantities. The all-time record for sales to date is held, perhaps surprisingly, by Franco Zeffirelli's *Romeo and Juliet*. Greta Garbo led in the long term stakes even before the recent revival of her sound films, with Marlene Dietrich as a somewhat laggard second. There is a continuing and increasing demand for silent films, and not only the classics. Less conventional

* Unless otherwise indicated, quotations in this section are from an article by Sheila Whitaker in the *Journal of the Society of Film and Television Arts*, Spring 1970.

requests are received from time to time from those whose interest
is less in the artistic or historic value of a particular film than in the
fact that it has incidental scenes (and stills) involving high-heeled
boots, leather clothing, schoolgirls in uniform and other fashion-
able fetishes. While the department cannot censor the use made
of it, it is naturally more concerned to promote the educational
application of its collection by providing slides and film strips for
schools and making special charges for educational purposes.

On the back of each still is stamped a warning that no reproduction rights go with the sale. Copyright has to be cleared with
the owner – generally the distributor but, as in the case of the films
themselves, sometimes difficult to trace, particularly in the case of
the earlier productions.

There have sometimes been complaints that the charge for
copies is high, but even so the department makes no profit and
would be unable to function were it not for its subsidy from the
Institute funds. Apart from the cost of storage space, and the staff
needed for filing, cataloguing, preserving and dealing with pur-
chasers, there is the fact that very often a negative will have to be
made of a particular still before the positive required can be
printed. Of the 700,000 prints in the collection, only some 53,000
have as yet been transferred to negatives. In the great majority of
cases, too, only a single copy is asked for, and this is far more
costly than, for instance, in the case of a fan club for a particular
star, where up to 500 copies of a photograph can be printed at one
time.

As with the Archive's film collection, there is the constant
balance to be considered between preservation and reproduction.
"The balance is very difficult to achieve fully, and inevitably it
can only be maintained by the provision of sufficient funds. For
example, at present the original stills are viewed and handled by
the public, with consequent damage, deterioration and sometimes
even theft. Owing to the enormous cost of the exercise, we have
not yet been able to carry out the most important preservation
requirement, namely to copy the entire collection on to negative
materials and provide only reference copies for the public to use.
In this way the content of the stills could be preserved and reproduced for many generations to come. We are not even able to

clean stills on acquisition to prevent fading due to excess hypo deposit, and as negatives are only made to order (i.e. for reproduction) some items may fade completely and be lost." It is obviously desirable that the department should possess its own photographic and reproductive facilities, and this is planned for the future. At present all the work has to be farmed out, with consequent increase in both the time and money needed to supply copies.

In addition to the stills there are also small but growing poster and slide collections, plans for colour reproduction to meet the probability that colour stills will increase to match colour films, and a Stills Hire Service, restricted to such concerns as film societies, educational bodies and libraries, at a rate of 5p per still per week.

4. THE INTERNATIONAL FEDERATION OF FILM ARCHIVES

*"The National Film Archive was created in London in May 1935, as the result of recommendations published in 1932. In June 1935 Iris Barry and John Abbott inaugurated the Museum of Modern Art's Film Department in New York. Einar Lauritzen in Stockholm had already started the private collection which was absorbed into the Swedish Technical Museum as Filmhistorika Samlingarna (Film History Collection). Henri Langlois was storing films in his mother's house, and beginning the film performances which were to be incorporated in 1936 as the Cinémathèque Français. Berlin had its Reichsfilmarchiv.

"In 1938, the four archives of London, New York, Paris and Berlin, recognising their need for mutual collaboration, formed the International Federation of Film Archives (FIAF) with headquarters in Paris. Its first Congress was held in New York in 1939.

"The development of FIAF was at once arrested by the outbreak of war. Contact with the Berlin Reichfilmarchiv was lost, and by the end of the war it had been destroyed and its collection dispersed. Contact with the Cinémathèque Français was lost with the Occupation, although Langlois, to his great credit, succeeded

* From an article by Ernest Lindgren in the *Journal of the Society of Film and Television Arts*, Spring 1970.

Erich von Stroheim arrives to open a twelve-week season of his films at the National Film Theatre in 1954. Frank Hazell, General Manager of the NFT is on the left

Erich von Stroheim with George Pearson, pioneer of British film production, and Arthur Dulay, silent film pianist at the NFT since its opening

Peter Ustinov at the NFT, with S. C. Roberts, Chairman of the
BFI 1952–56

Luis Buñuel at the NFT
during its Telekinema days

in holding it together until Paris was liberated. In 1946 the surviving founder members (National Film Archive, Museum of Modern Art Film Department and Cinémathèque Français) came together in Paris to revive the Federation, which immediately began to attract new members. In the early sixties the FIAF faced its most serious crisis in an internal clash between the principles of autocratic and democratic control. Democracy won, and Henri Langlois most regrettably took the Cinémathèque out of FIAF. Happily, the unity of FIAF was not otherwise seriously disturbed and its growth continued without interruption.

"Today FIAF, with thirty-five members in twenty-nine countries (Albania, Australia, Austria, Belgium, Bulgaria, Canada, Cuba, Czechoslovakia, Denmark, Finland, France, West Germany, East Germany, Great Britain, Holland, Hungary, India, Israel, Italy, Norway, Poland, Portugal, Rumania, Spain, Sweden, Turkey, USA, USSR, and Yugoslavia) is the largest and strongest of all international film organisations, certainly in the cultural field. . . .

"All the members of the Federation come together in a General Meeting and Congress once a year . . . and between General Meetings control is exercised by its Executive Committee. The Federation is entirely non-political and independent, being financed solely by the contributions of its members.

"The functions of FIAF are several. It facilitates communication and exchange between its members. It also maintains in its Statutes and Rules a common code of conduct for all its member archives. They hold in their collections films of which they do not own the copyright, and which they have no right to use outside their own premises without the authorisation of the copyright owners, who are normally producing and distributing (or transmitting) companies. They are also dependent on these companies for further films to add to their collections. No genuine archive, therefore, would want to use any of its films against the commercial interests of the owners of the rights, because this would endanger its existence at its own national level. But even if an archive were to act irresponsibly, there is the further sanction which FIAF can apply at the international level, of expelling it from membership – outlawing it, in effect, from the international archive movement. . .

F

"Fundamentally, perhaps, what gives FIAF its strength, and makes it more than an international talking shop, is the fact that all its members, however they may vary in status or size or maturity, are engaged in a severely practical task in an entirely new field, and facing many problems which no-one has had to deal with before. In trying to solve these problems in their own countries, they find themselves to a large degree isolated. Only by coming together internationally are they able to find the community of interests, the moral support and the exchange of experience and ideas, which they need to sustain them in their own national effort. FIAF justifies itself by providing this international meeting point, and it is held together by the very practical nature of the work which its members require it to undertake."

In 1968, to celebrate the 30th anniversary of the FIAF a season of films contributed by its members was held at the National Film Theatre during the week of the 24th Annual Congress, which was opened on 23rd May by H.R.H. Princess Margaret, Countess of Snowden. The sixteen programmes included *Y Mañana* (Belgium), *Extase* (Czechoslovakia), *Seven Footprints to Satan* (Denmark), *Elokuu* (Finland), four versions of *Der Hauptmann von Köpenick* (Germany), *Three Days and a Child* (Israel), *Maciste Alpino* (Italy), *Diminetile Unui Baiat Cuminte* (Rumania) *Mysteriet Natten Till Den 25:e* (Sweden), *Lady of the Pavements* (USA), *October* (USSR), a programme of British fiction films 1898–1910, shorts from Austria, Canada and Holland, and the work of the pioneer animator Winsor McCay, creator of *Gertie the Dinosaur*.

3

Education

When the BFI was formed in 1933 with so large an emphasis on its functions as an adviser to develop the use of *film* in *education*, the consideration that there might be an equally valid reason for encouraging the development of *education* in *film* would probably have been dismissed as of secondary, even trivial importance. Almost from the start, however, this inevitably became one of its provinces, when lectures were inaugurated to publish its aims and increase membership. As early as 1934, Ernest Lindgren was giving talks at the City Literary Institute and elsewhere on the film – not primarily as a commercial form of mass entertainment, nor as an additional teacher's aid in the classroom, but as a creative medium worthy of consideration in its own right. Summer schools, too, annual fortnightly residential courses in what was then known as film appreciation, are nearly as old as the Institute itself. Up to the time of the Radcliffe Report, however, these were mainly ancillary activities not regarded as ends in themselves.

The Report, as we have seen, shifted the emphasis away from the *films-in-schools* responsibilities which had so far circumscribed the Institute's possibilities of expansion, and opened the way for recognition of the cinema as a subject for serious study. Even so, developments were slow in getting started, and it was not until Stanley Reed joined the Institute in 1950 that any serious steps were taken. To avoid any appearance of wishing to challenge the functions of the Committee for Visual Aids in Education, a post of Film Appreciation Officer was created, filled first by Reed, then by Tony Hodgkinson, and in 1957 by Paddy Whannel. It was felt, however, that the word 'appreciation' had an old-fashioned ring about it, and was too limited in its meaning. "It understated the importance of knowledge. It was a limited, critical term, and there is a lot more to understanding a film than criticism," Whannel considers, and shortly after he took over, the title of Education Department was adopted. "The work of the Department is based on the belief that the cinema, a great contemporary art and one of the powerful media operating in society, must find its place in the curriculum. The department thus exists primarily to service teachers and lecturers who are concerned to introduce and pursue this work."* In this capacity it offers advice and materials to those conducting courses in film – and in television – and arranges individual lectures and sessions on their behalf.

Believing that a valuable method of learning to understand film is to learn how to make them, the department encourages this, and will also where possible provide – or at least advise on the obtaining of – the necessary equipment. Film-making is now a recognised activity in many schools and colleges, in some as a hobby, in others integrated into the film course. The aim, it is emphasised, is not to train future professional film-makers, but to encourage young people to handle the tools of the art as they might handle paint or clay. Film courses are seen as a part of a general liberal education – as significant a part as those in literature or music – not as practical training such as would be given at a film school, though the department also contributes lectures to such bodies as the London Film School and the Royal College of Art.

Recognition of the significance and influence of film and tele-vision was expressed in the Newsom Report on Education of 1963: "Here we should wish to add a strong claim for the study of film and television in their own right, as powerful forces in our culture and significant sources of language and ideas. Although the study of these media has for some time been accepted in a small number of schools as an important part of the curriculum, in the majority of schools they are used only as visual aids for the presentation of material connected with other subjects. . . . The most important and most general use of these media, however, as major means for the mass communication of cultural experience, is not generally dealt with in schools any more than it is in colleges or universities. Little attention is paid to the degree to which film

* Services to Education, BFI Publications.

and television enter into and influence the lives of our pupils and to these media as legitimate means for the communication of personal experience alongside literature, music and painting.

"The culture provided by all the mass media, but particularly by film and television, represents the most significant environmental factor that teachers have to take into account."

An important change of approach to the subject began to make itself felt a few years ago and was noted in *Film Teaching*, a pamphlet devoted to film study within the field of education: "Without abandoning the historical approach or minimising its value, there has been a notable shift towards critical analysis, to the study in detail of particular films, frequently drawn from the contemporary cinema. There is now less emphasis on imparting information about how a film is made and more on the mutual discussion of meaning and value. The kind of information now provided is designed more intimately to illuminate the response to the individuality and to the variety of particular films."

In 1964, with the taking over by the Department of Education and Science from the Treasury of responsibility for financing the BFI, the Education Department received an increased grant which enabled it to increase its staff and expand its services.

During the late fifties a special promotional effort was made with the colleges of further education, and this later bore fruit in Berkshire College (formerly Bulmershe), Reading; Bede College of Education, Durham; Madeley College, and Alnwick College of Education, which now offer the art of film as a main course for students. Contacts have also been made at university level, and attempts are continuing towards the development of this work, though there is a gap between the growth of interest among students and younger lecturers, and the achievement of institutional support. Links are maintained with the work proceeding abroad, through the International Centre of Films for Children and Young People, the Centre International de Liaison des Ecoles de Cinéma et de Télévision, and by attendances at various film education conferences.

The most ambitious undertaking of the Education Department to date is the three-to-four year University of London extramural certificate and diploma course. The student takes intermediary examinations at the end of the first two years, and a final at the end of the third. If he passes this he receives a Certificate in Film Study. Thereafter, provided his grades are high enough, he can work for a diploma – possibly by making a film himself, more usually by writing a thesis on some particular aspect of the subject – in a fourth and final year. The Education Department has direct responsibility for providing the four courses, each of which has twenty-four sessions. The subjects for 1969–70 were:

Films and Criticism

History and Development of the Cinema

The Director's Cinema

John Ford and the American Cinema

Apart from this, there are in various universities and colleges the first beginnings of academic study – perhaps the most advanced being the Polytechnic of Central London (the Regent Street Polytechnic), where a three-year course in the photographic arts, covering both still photography and film production, leads to the ordinary degree of bachelor of arts.

Despite these advances, there is still need for more substantial forms of training. Many teachers interested in developing some kind of work in film feel hampered by lack of experience and knowledge. "The best teaching of film, as indeed the best teaching in any of the arts, is done by those excited by the medium. They will be enthusiasts. They will know the cinema's greatest works, but they will also go to the movies because they like the experience. They will accept without question that Buñuel, Renoir, Ozu, Wajda and the other great directors are major creative artists equal in stature to those working in other fields. They will respond to the great popular genres of Hollywood as art rather than social documents. As teachers they will not be thinking in the defensive terms suggested by a phrase like *counterbalancing assistance*, but will be seeking to open their pupils to receive the best experience the cinema has to offer. In other words, the cinema is worthy of study in its own right. Educationalists at all levels within formal education are beginning to realise that the study of film can be as rewarding and as complex a discipline as the more accepted studies of literature and painting."*

* *Outlook 1966.*

But enthusiasm without training or knowledge does not make a teacher. "The difficulties here are inevitable," Paddy Whannel comments, "and the solutions long term. Most of the work of the BFI Education Department and SEFT* is designed to improve the situation."

A second difficulty facing the film teacher is that of availability of his materials.† "A great many important films are not available from any source . . . this is not crucial at the school level, but at the higher levels of education it is crippling to specialized work and makes virtually impossible the comprehensive study of the films of any one director.

"Some of the films not available commercially are held by the National Film Archive, but in general at present the Archive holds only a small proportion of the films of any one director and there are many important directors not represented at all. Moreover the Archive films can only be seen on BFI premises and where only one copy is held (which is usual) this cannot be projected but seen only on a table viewer.

"There are two main reasons why films are not available – commercial and contractual. Many films have not been bought by distributors because it did not seem commercially worthwhile to do so or they may have been withdrawn from distribution because it seemed that their commercial life was over. Other films have been withdrawn for various contractual reasons, the rights may have been taken up by television or the rights may have expired and the copyright owners are asking for terms that no distributor will meet."

The problem is a formidable one, with no solution at present

* SEFT, the Society for Education in Film and Television, is a voluntary body of practising teachers and others who are interested in the promotion of screen education. Its members are drawn from several levels of education, including primary schools, all types of secondary schools, colleges of education and others. Its publications include occasional pamphlets, and a quarterly magazine *Screen*, devoted to developing film study in depth and at the same time providing a source of film teaching services and materials. SEFT holds its own summer school, and arranges viewing sessions for teachers in London and the provinces.

† The following quotations are taken from two articles by Paddy Whannel in the SEFT magazine *Screen*, Vol. 10, Nos. 1 and 3.

in sight which would not involve very great expense of time and money and might even then prove abortive.

Apart from the difficulty of obtaining the films themselves there is the cumbersome nature of the apparatus required to show them – not only the projectors themselves (complex, heavy and easily damaged precision machines), but the need for suitable room for screen, speakers, power supply, and the difficulty in these all-glass-wall days of achieving total darkness.

Alongside such practical problems, as Paddy Whannel points out, "there is the theoretical issue of defining the content of the subject and reaching some agreement about its methods of study.

"To take a very simple example, decision makers in education (headmasters, principals, education officers, etc.) will only make provision for film study courses if they have a clear understanding of what the subject is and why it is relevant and important. It is still true that in most quarters this understanding does not exist. That it doesn't cannot be put down to academic conservatism alone. The fact that there is no agreed term to describe the subject, no equivalent of the term 'literature' for example, is the most obvious indication of the difficulty. All of us shift uneasily between such descriptions as Film Education, with the danger of confusing the subject with audio-visual aids, and the clumsy Screen Education, implying the uncertain and dubious inclusion of television. At times, for the sake of clarity, we are even driven to return to the old-fashioned term, Film Appreciation, with all its limiting connotations. . . .

"We have to argue first of all for the *idea* of the study of film as art and entertainment as a distinct discipline having its own particular problems. Secondly, we need to establish centres at all levels in education, but especially within higher education, where such a study can take place. The general case for Film Study is best put in these terms: the cinema is a significant feature of contemporary culture representing the most developed and distinctive form of art produced by technology with the unique feature that its growth, from its most primitive beginnings, is preserved for study on celluloid."

Finally, on the need for feature films – the 'ordinary' films of fiction as seen in commercial and specialist cinemas – to be made more readily available for study, Whannel sums up: "Two things need to be driven home to the education authorities and other decision makers within education. The first of these is that for the new approaches to teaching, especially in the humanities, the traditional education film is of little relevance and that teachers are seeking films which have not been designed for educational use and are not to be found in the educational film libraries. The second is the need to recognize that it is in the feature film that the techniques of visual communication are to be seen at their most expressive and imaginative. Artists like Buñuel, Bergman, Ozu, Renoir and Ford are the cinema's equivalent of the great novelists and dramatists. At present no substantial provision is made in higher education for the study of their work. It is urgent that such provision be made, otherwise advances in educational technology will be superficial and the use of film in education will remain at a primitive level."

Lecture Service

Although the giving of lectures was a part of the Institute's activities since its formation, when Clifford Collinson set out to publicise its purpose and Ernest Lindgren and others gave talks on various aspects of the cinema both in London and the provinces, it was not until 1948, following the Radcliffe Report, that a proposal was made to set up an official Lecture Service under a co-ordinating officer. Hitherto lecturers had been drawn almost entirely from the BFI staff, but with the widening scope of its activities there was a feeling that a more representative service should be set up, under the Education Department, with a panel drawn from various sides of the industry, and from the teaching profession, as well as from the Institute itself. This task was under the supervision of Stanley Reed, in his capacity of the first Film Appreciation Officer. In 1953 the post of Lecturer Officer was taken over by Molly Lloyd, who had joined the BFI as Stanley Reed's secretary, and she has held this office ever since.

The very large increase in the demand for lecturers is shown by the following table:

	BFI Staff Lecturer	Panel	Total
1948–59			Less than 40
1958–59			602
1963–64	340	691	1,031
1964–65	440	701	1,141
1965–66	559	431	790*
1966–67	305	444	749
1967–68	240	498	738
1968–69	233	654	887
1969–70	267	737	1,004

Many of the Institute departments staff take on assignments in their spare time.

At present there are between 80 and 90 lecturers on the panel, but of these only some forty are really active, many others having little time, and a few having less inclination. "All the members are accredited speakers," says Miss Lloyd, "and whenever possible we try to sit in on talks given by newcomers."

Frequently a film celebrity not on the panel will be requested as a speaker by a film society or educational group, and whenever possible this is arranged. People connected with the industry such as Bryan Forbes, Mai Zetterling, Peter Sellers, Joseph Losey, Carl Foreman, Sylvia Syms, Clive Donner and John Trevelyan have frequently given lectures in such cases and have expressed their willingness to be invited at any time, though they are not (with the exception of Clive Donner) on the panel. All enquirers for 'big names' are warned that if the speaker should have to drop out – generally because of a sudden film commitment – it is unlikely that anyone of equal eminence will be obtainable at short notice. It is always possible, of course, that the less prominent substitute may turn out to be the better speaker.

On enquiry, an application form is sent requesting such details as single lecture or course, duration, subject, anticipated attendance figures, type of audience, and equipment available. A fee is charged varying according to the audience, the speaker, the time spent in travelling, etc., and some organisations, such as the uni-

* Change of policy whereby the provincial lecturers booked their own films for established courses.

versities, have a fixed scale. An agency commission is deducted from the lecturer's fee, and all arrangements, including travelling, are handled on his behalf.

Of prime importance in any talk on the cinema is the availability of films and, in particular, of film extracts. The Service issues a list of suggested topics, including only those which can be illustrated in this way. There can be difficulties – when, for instance, a lecture is asked for on one of the Eastern European or South American countries, or on modern Germany, where films are difficult to obtain. Other subjects occasionally requested, e.g. method acting, cannot be satisfactorily illustrated. In general, however, the majority of subjects can be covered. The Lecture Service holds its own collection of extracts, all of which are supplied free of charge to BFI Lecturers. Feature films are obtained either from the Distribution Library or from commercial distributors through the Central Booking Agency, at the normal booking fees, the CBA signing a contract on the lecturer's behalf and, in the case of sessions outside London, arranging for the posting of the films.

The extracts catalogue is a comprehensive one, listing films from early Chaplin comedies to last year's productions. It includes not only expected classics such as *The Birth of a Nation*, *Citizen Kane*, *Richard III* and *The Third Man* but also less 'important' films, and such rarities as the early English sound revue *Elstree Calling*, a Rin Tin Tin feature, and the 1913 *Pickwick Papers*. Foreign films are strongly represented, Godard, Bergman, Buñuel, early Russian and German classics, etc., and – in the case of sound films – wherever possible in sub-titled versions. There is a selection of television programmes such as *Culloden*, and episodes from *Z Cars* and *Dr Who*. There are over 600 in all, lasting from about six to twenty minutes, supplied with brief programme notes. A list of suggested topics includes Animation, Comedy, Editing, Film Criticism, Horror, New Wave, Propaganda and the Cinema, individual countries and directors. Certain subjects undergoing a phase of popularity (Hitchcock, a perennial, Bergman, a past perennial, French Cinema, Horror) have to be booked a long period in advance.

Comprehensive courses are also provided, ranging from high

level courses such as those arranged for the London University Extra-Mural Department to week-end schools for teachers, youth leaders and film societies. These are planned to fit the requirements of the audience and the point of view of the lecturer. Typical examples are:

Films and Criticism – twelve or twenty-four sessions. A general course on the cinema which places the emphasis on aesthetics rather than on film history, mainly in detailed studies of individual films and directors. Films include *Birth of a Nation*, *Strike*, *Foolish Wives*, *La Grande Illusion*, *Citizen Kane*, and *Living*.

The Art of the Film – twelve or twenty-four sessions. A general course with the emphasis on film history from early days up to the present, including individual sessions on specialist aspects such as film economics, the use of sound, screen acting, etc.

The Cinema and Education – six or ten sessions. A course specially planned for educationalists, covering the creative side, film criticism and economics, with special attention to the sociology of cinema and the young audience.

Making Movies – a week-end school. A short course on the main creative elements in films and the problems of response and criticism.

One of the longest standing and most interesting engagements is that conducted by the Merseyside Film Institute Society. For the past sixteen years or so the society has been conducting a series of film appreciation lectures for the senior forms of grammar schools and technical colleges of the area. On one day in the last week of each school term about 3,000 boys and girls between the ages of fifteen and eighteen attend either a morning or an afternoon session at the Liverpool Philharmonic Hall. There they are shown a film, outstanding of its kind, preceded by a talk. In the course of each year the society tries to provide two film-makers and one critic to address the audience. Over the years the speakers have included Dilys Powell, Roger Manvell, Arnot Robertson, Ronald Neame, T. E. B. Clarke, Charles Frend, John Grierson, Yvonne Mitchell, David Kossoff, Guy Hamilton, Carl Foreman, Muir Mathieson, Jacques Brunius and John Halas. Films screened include *The Overlanders, Hue and Cry, Great Expectations, Oliver Twist, Passport to Pimlico, Scott of the Antarctic, Seven Days to Noon, The Young Mr Lincoln* and *Morning Departure.* "Care has been exercised in the selection of films," states a circular issued a few years ago, "in that we do not offend religious or racial susceptibilities in our very cosmopolitan city and avoid the type of sentiment that appears ludicrous to the adolescent" – which must present problems today.

Lectures are often in demand for less conventional places than film societies or educational establishments. One of the most successful series was held over a number of years at monthly intervals in Wandsworth Prison. "It was never difficult to find people willing to undertake this assignment," Miss Lloyd says. "Bryan Forbes, in fact, almost adopted the prisoners, and used to send feature films to be shown at Easter and Christmas at his own expense." The Wandsworth audience was composed of a rehabilitation group of men due to leave the prison in about twelve months. All the arranging of the session, the booking of the film, the setting up of the hall, the writing of programme notes, the reception and chairing of the speaker, was done by the men themselves. Any subject was welcome, and no censorship was imposed by the authorities. Sometimes a prison officer sat in on the lectures, but very often it was attended only by the prisoners themselves. In every instance a personal letter of thanks was sent by the men to the lecturer involved. Another prison at which lectures were regularly given was Maidstone. Unfortunately, when the tighter security of prisons came under scrutiny in recent years, visitors in general to prisons were cut down, but it is still looked upon as an important part of the Lecture Service's functions should it ever be required. Only one stipulation was made by the authorities – the lecturer must come on his own. If he turns up on the doorstep with an unexpected companion, however mild in appearance, he was apt to be looked at slightly askance. So the advice given to lecturers is: if you want to take your wife with you, ring up first.

Lecturing on film, wherever it takes place, can involve anxieties not met with in connection with staider subjects. There are, to start with, the practical conditions with which he may be suddenly and appallingly faced. An illustrated talk on the horror film, for instance, can lose most of its effect if the extracts are projected in half-daylight, with a reassuring sun peeping through curtains gingerly fastened together with bent safety-pins. A subtle, low-toned drama is not at its best if the subtle, highly charged dialogue comes croaking inaudibly out of an inadequate speaker placed to one side of the screen on a greengrocer's wooden box. And even when conditions are good (and to be fair, they are generally not bad), there is always the personal angle to be wary of. Lecture on the properties of a chemical substance and, whatever the audience may feel about it, the facts are there: talk about a film, and whatever theories are expounded reactions will inevitably vary with the individual. This is, of course, all as it should be. Even so, it can be disheartening, after dwelling at length on the incomparable humour of a great comedian and then showing a side-splitting example of his work, to be met with a glum-faced "Well, it didn't make *me* laugh," – or, even worse, as the final scream dies away in a thriller which has left the lecturer's voice still uncertain from sheer terror, to hear a scornful "It'd take more than that to frighten *me*!" Dilys Powell has said, "One man's *frisson* is another's guffaw."

Summer Schools

These are held annually by the Education Department on a fortnightly residential basis, in different parts of the country, with BFI lecturers augmented by visits from workers in the film industry. The tone and intent of the schools have altered radically with the passing of time. In the early days, in fact up to the late fifties, they were general in character, with a wide range of subjects treated on a fairly popular level. They were held always in the same place – the University of Bangor – and the aim was to obtain big names as visiting lecturers who would attract those interested in the cinema in the widest sense. Speakers such as Orson Welles, Mai Zetterling, Sir Michael Redgrave, Anthony Asquith, Sir Michael Balcon, Max Ophuls, Carl Foreman, William Alwyn, John Grierson, Compton Mackenzie, Lotte Reiniger, Lindsay Anderson, Carl Dreyer, Bessie Love, Walter

Wanger, Michael Powell, Charles Frend, Bridget Boland, to name but a few, testify to the Department's success in this aim. With the increase of a deeper and more specialised study of the films, however, especially by young people, a need was felt to make the course of a kind to correspond more closely with this development. Nowadays one whole season will be devoted to, say, the Western, to surrealism, to some particular director, to film criticism. It follows that there has been a change in the type of guest lecturer, who is more likely now to be someone who can make a direct contribution to the theme of the course, rather than a celebrity *per se*.

Entrants for the schools are enrolled by the Lecture Service, and number between seventy and eighty, this having been found the most convenient size for dividing up into teams for practical film-making. There is no age limit, but applicants under eighteen are not encouraged. A surprisingly large proportion of older applications are received, and in recent years the number of teachers anxious to attend has grown considerably. Whenever necessary these are given priority and frequently they are able to obtain grants from the local education authority for the course. This, in fact, in Stanley Reed's view, is the real significance of the Summer Schools. "It is important for us to encourage training colleges and universities to do this sort of thing themselves, rather than leave it for the students always to come to us. Our job really is to prepare other people to do the job, and to persuade educational bodies to take film studies into their curriculum at both university and primary school level. Apart from this, the Schools serve a useful purpose in enabling the lecture staff of the BFI to get together for a fortnight in the year after working on their own during the rest of the time."

The programme is an arduous one, consisting of lectures in the morning, film-making (voluntary) in the afternoon, and watching feature films in the evening and often into the small hours of the following day. Film shot during one day is sent to London, processed overnight and despatched back again the following day so that the different teams can see as quickly as possible the work they have already done. On the last night of the School all the different units screen their efforts. All equipment, cameras, film stock, editing material, etc. is provided, the charge being included in the fee.

As the emphasis shifted from popular to more specialised programmes, it began to become apparent also that the School should be held in different parts of the country, rather than returning each time to Bangor. Consequently in recent years it has taken place in widely separated places – Bath, Ripon, Birmingham, Hoddesdon, St Andrews, Eastbourne, and elsewhere – choice of district being, of course, governed by the availability of suitable accommodation. One of the most successful fortnights was held in Scotland in conjunction with the Scottish Film Council, during the Edinburgh Festival. For the first week members stayed in Glasgow University, and for the second moved over to Edinburgh. "We lost quite a lot of people during the second week," says Miss Lloyd, "because they went off to see the Festival events in the evenings, but at least it made for variety. The first week was under strict tuition, the second much more sociable, the only disadvantage being that the friendly atmosphere of everyone being together in a hall of residence during the first week was dissipated in the scattered accommodation which was all that was available at the time in Edinburgh."

That particular fortnight was also made memorable by a visit from the inimitable Jacques Tati, in Edinburgh for the Festival, and by a wire which – when the Tattoo and other festivities were over and he had returned to Paris – was received at the Institute: "TA-TA TATTOO, TATI".

The opening of the National Film Theatre's own building, October 1957, by HRH Princess Margaret. Left to right: G. A. Smith, 94-year-old British cinema pioneer; Akira Kurosawa; Vittoria de Sica; Gina Lollobrigida; John Ford; HRH Princess Margaret; Sir Laurence Olivier

The original entrance of NFT 1
Auditorium of NFT 1 showing the screen and tabs

uditorium of NFT 2 show-
ing the projection box

rphone commentary in use
r foreign-language films at
NFT

Orson Welles at a BFI Summer School, with Denis Forman

Sylvester Gates, Stanley Reed and James Quinn at the opening of the third London Film Festival, 1959

Stanley Reed presenting Sophia Loren with the Korda Star Award given by the BFI for services to the popular cinema, 1965

4

Presentation

History

The National Film Theatre is the main channel of communication between the Institute and its members; for some, in fact,
it is probably their only connection, except when they post their
subscriptions each year. It is the activity most in the public eye,
and is actually open to that public at present every Saturday, and
during the London Film Festival. The absolute necessity of a film
institute owning a film theatre is so obvious it seems incredible
that it should have had to wait – for lack of funds – nearly twenty
years before it acquired one. It is now, however, as comprehensive
as any of its kind in the world. The story of the search for such a
building and of the BFI's early association with the Festival of
Britain Telekinema has been outlined in the first part of this book,
so that we can take up the account from the moment when, with
the closing of the Exhibition, the National Film Theatre could at
last be said to have become a reality.

When its function as part of the Festival of Britain came to an
end the Telekinema, which was a handsome building in contemporary style and not just the customary exhibition framework,
was re-equipped as a repertory cinema of some 400 seats and club
premises, with stereo equipment and projectors on both 16mm
and 35mm gauges capable of screening old films at their proper
speed and adapting their gates to any size of frame. A separate
committee was formed for the setting up of the NFT, to which a
number of members of the industry, including Cecil Bernstein,
were judiciously appointed. From the start it was established as a
'club' cinema, free from censorship, and was able to import films
without paying duty. Finance for the opening was provided by a

G

grant from the British Film Production Board through the co-operation of the film industry.

There was a special premiere programme for 24th October – 8th November 1952, when it opened its doors under the management of Frank Hazell, who remained as General Manager until 1958. The films included Anthony Asquith's *Pygmalion*, a Personality Review featuring Garbo, Chaplin, Buster Keaton, Stroheim, Marlene Dietrich, Laurence Olivier, Mary Pickford and others, and a group of Norman McLaren's experimental and stereoscopic animation work. "In arranging the initial programmes for the theatre," writes Denis Forman*, "the Institute had three objectives in view; first, to present a steady repertory of the acknowledged masterpieces of the screen; second, to concentrate attention on some theme of contemporary interest or importance in the cinema, and thirdly (in keeping with the traditions of the Telekinema), to demonstrate what was new and experimental. Thus two nights every week were devoted to a chronological survey of film history under the general title of *Fifty Years of Film*, four nights in each week were given to a series of studies of the work of outstanding directors, or else to some decisive trend in the cinema, past or present."

One of the earliest seasons devoted to a single director was, as might have been expected, Alfred Hitchcock – then, as now, sure box office. Others ranged from early silents to Vittorio de Sica, including, besides *Bicycle Thieves* and *Umberto D*, some of the Italian master's less familiar work. There was also an Ealing Comedy series. For the first Christmas season the theatre was dressed up and rechristened 'The Bijou', showing a typical 1915 programme.†

The year 1954 featured von Stroheim, as actor and director, from *Greed* to *Queen Kelly* and *Sunset Boulevard*, and (in a season of Asian productions) what was described as the only 'commercial' Japanese film to have been shown in this country, *The Imposter*, directed by Tatsuo Osone.

A *Homage to United Artists* series in 1955 started with a number of screenings of Chaplin's *The Gold Rush*. The most notable

* *The Film and the Public.*

† The brief survey of programmes in the following pages can only be selective: a complete list of NFT seasons is given in the appendix.

events of the year were comprehensive surveys of the work of John Ford and Luis Buñuel. A practice of those days, fortunately later abandoned, was to run the Saturday showings (then as now open to the public) on a 'continuous performance' basis, a custom out of keeping with the NFT's avowed attitude of respect towards the art it promoted.

The next year, 1956, included another Hitchcock season (he had been presented on occasions throughout) and salutes to Warner Brothers and to the twenty-first anniversary of Rank Distributors. Around this year, also, the policy began to turn, increasingly towards the present. In January two important seasons were presented – important not only in themselves but as the beginning of a new trend: *New Activity* and *Free Cinema One*. *"*New Activity* was the NFT's first attempt to bring London new films from abroad, films which had been neglected by commercial distributors, the "Cinderellas of the Film Festivals". There is no need now to explain what *Free Cinema* was – the term has entered film history. But in 1956, it meant Lindsay Anderson's *O Dreamland*, Tony Richardson's and Karel Reisz's *Momma Don't Allow*, and Lorenza Mazzetti's *Together*. . . .

"Encouraged by the success of this 'New Activity', the NFT went on in the same year to present the British premier of *Pather Panchali*, *Free Cinema Two* and a comprehensive Russian Panorama – which included new films as well as old. The year ended with Derek Prouse's great Italian season, introducing to Londoners the films of Visconti, Maselli, Rossi and Fellini and, with a comprehensive season devoted to new French shorts, including works by many young directors who have since become world-famous." The last year in the old home, 1957, ranged widely from Sam Goldwyn to Max Ophuls, Yugoslavia to Associated Rediffusion Documentaries, Bogart to East German Scene.

Attendances at the Telekinema during the four complete years of its NFT existence were:

1953	159,157
1954	181,905
1955	202,714
1956	222,644

* *The First Ten Years*, NFT Booklet (1962).

Spectacular as the success of the ex-Festival building was, however, it was known from the start that the arrangement could be only a temporary one. Apart from the fact that it was only held on a temporary lease, there were various drawbacks in the building itself. There was no possibility of expansion, seating arrangements were imperfect, projection facilities were limited – it could not, for instance, take in the new wide screen films, and last but not least it was designed originally, despite its solidity, for a summertime exhibition, and there were no adequate arrangements for heating the auditorium. Almost as soon as the first season was under way there began the tortuous planning, budgeting and negotiating with the LCC (as the GLC was then called) for a more permanent home. First proposals (in 1953) for full-size Institute premises on the South Bank, incorporating a film theatre in one building, had to be abandoned as too costly: two years later the idea was born of constructing an auditorium under one of the arches of Waterloo Bridge. The building was designed by the council's own Architects Department under N. W. Engleback, who exercised considerable ingenuity in moulding the building into the space available. A major problem was the exclusion of noise from the traffic-laden bridge overhead. Complaints also began to come in shortly after the opening regarding unsatisfactory heating and accoustics, and in fact over a period considerable difficulties were encountered over insulation in general. Fortunately fire precaution demands necessitated a rule – for which it is impossible to feel sufficient gratitude – of No Smoking.

The single-tier auditorium seats some 500, in a rather wider arc than might seem desirable – though care has been taken in the relative placing of screen and seats, to minimise side-distortion as much as possible. The projection room extends over the auditorium, and adjoining this is a small private cinema (which it also serves and which, until the building of the new extensions in 1969–70, overhung the main entrance to the cinema. The projection equipment was, and is, one of the most complete and complex in the world, incorporating facilities for accommodating ten different picture ratios, and speed changes to anything between 16 and 25 frames per second. In addition there is provision for spoken commentaries to accompany foreign-language films which lack subtitles. (see p. 120). Alf Francis, chief projectionist, who has been with the NFT since its first opening at the Tele-kinema, has under him a staff of ten to run both the main theatre and its younger brother, NFT 2. The most notable features of the decor are the screen tabs – jazzy black-and-gold metal grilles which fold and unfold across the screen by a rolling device. They provide a lighthearted motif in a somewhat austere (but far from gloomy) scheme of decoration, and were sadly missed during a temporary absence when they were replaced by a pair of (appa-rently) left-over blackout curtains.

In February 1957 Princess Margaret had visited the Telekinema and had expressed her willingness to open the new building in due course. The ceremony took place on 15th October of the same year, and was a gala occasion. Leading film directors from four countries – René Clair, John Ford, Vittorio de Sica and (in national Japanese costume) Akira Kurosawa – were present. Among other celebrities were Gina Lollobrigida and G. A. Smith, 94 years of age and a pioneer of the British cinema. A number of film-makers received presentations, the awards being made by Lord Hailsham – then Lord President of the Council – and Sir Laurence Olivier read the citations. Among the films proposed for the opening ceremony were the Japanese version (very far re-moved) of Macbeth, *Throne of Blood*, Anthony Asquith's *Orders to Kill*, *Woman in a Dressing Gown* and revivals of *49th Parallel* or *The Queen of Spades*. Finally it was decided to show, instead of a single feature, a compilation of film clips "illustrating the richness and diversity of the cinema." This was devised and put together by Lindsay Anderson and Derek Prouse.

The cinema started immediately with the first London Film Festival*, which lasted until 26th October and, being open to the public, helped to advertise its arrival.

Attendance figures covering the change of situation were:

1956	222,644
1957	203,640
1958	233,910,

and prices in the new theatre ranged from 2s 6d, 3s 6d, 4s, to 5s.
* See p. 129.

Programmes during its first complete year (1958) included films from Brussels and Central Europe, British comedies of the thirties (with a special section on the art of Will Hay), tributes to the Russian Theatre, Max Ophuls and Jean Cocteau. The year finished with an interesting experiment – a programme entitled 'The Lion's Roar', the story of M-G-M's thirty-five years of film production, screened entirely from 16mm prints.

The following year Leslie Hardcastle, after having worked previously in the Central Booking Agency and as assistant at the NFT, took over from Frank Hazell as General Manager, under Stanley Reed and John Huntley. Richard Roud was in charge of programme planning. In 1966 Hardcastle became Controller of the NFT, with complete executive power for running the theatre.

The highlight of 1959 was the season of Swedish films, "The Passionate Cinema", consisting mainly, as might be expected, of Ingmar Bergman (*Port of Call*, *Prison*, *Thirst*, *Summer Interlude*, *Waiting Women*, *Sawdust and Tinsel*, *A Lesson in Love*, *Smiles of a Summer Night*, *The Seventh Seal*, *Brink of Life*), but including also the work of other directors such as Alf Sjöberg (for whose *Frenzy* Bergman wrote the script), Arne Sucksdorff and Gustaf Molander. The season was accompanied by a very informative and attractive booklet compiled by John Gillett, long associated with the Institute as critic and Research Officer. Less happy was a major season on 'thirty Years of British Documentary', whose requiem was "timely but financially unrewarding". The BFI has always recognised the need to support this important and potentially exciting branch of the cinema, at which Britain has for so long excelled, but from which the public resolutely stay away (though it has admittedly come into its own in new ways on television). Another unusual season was 'The Negro World', presented in association with the Society of African Culture, and including feature films (*Hallelujah!*, *Intruder in the Dust*, *A Man is Ten Feet Tall*), documentaries, jazz, music and dance, and drama, introduced by celebrities such as Richard Wright, George Lamming and El Lasebikan. There was also a retrospective of the work of Robert Donat, who died in 1958, and the year drew to an end with an extremely successful comedy season, "100 Clowns", surveying the work of comedians from Mexico, Sweden, Czechoslovakia, Hungary, America and Britain, and contrasting the style of such artists as Nils Poppe, Jacques Tati, Keaton, Jerry Lewis, Harold Lloyd, the Marx Brothers, Will Hay and Cantinflas. Already this year proposals were being made regarding an extension of the building, which resulted in the opening – far, far ahead – of NFT 2. It was the start of a long and wearisome planning trek through what must have seemed at times a very dark tunnel with barely a glimmer of light at the end of it.

The following year, 1960, saw the restitution of the Archive Programmes of all-time classics, withdrawn some time previously because of a drop in attendance. One such film was screened each Monday night. The most notable season concerned France – the first full-scale review of the country's productions to be held at the NFT. It started with 1930 and tended to avoid the best-known films (except in extracts) in favour of those which, at that time, were less familiar: Renoir's *La Chienne*, Bresson's *Les Dames du Bois de Boulogne*, Clair's *Quattorze Juillet*, etc. The last part included an interesting group of productions made during the Occupation, such as Clouzot's *Le Corbeau*. This was followed by a selection of American 'New Wave' pictures under the general title "Beat Square and Cool", which might be regarded as a sort of forerunner of the Underground programmes ten years later.

The National Film Archive celebrated its Silver Jubilee with ten special programmes representing different aspects of its work in acquisition and preservation, including the very rare print of Douglas Fairbanks Snr's *The Black Pirate*, an extract from the first British colour feature *The Glorious Adventure*, the Russian 1916 and English 1948 versions of Pushkin's *The Queen of Spades*, and several programmes of rare shorts. Perhaps the year's most original venture was a brief Chinese season, the first of its kind to be arranged in the Western world.

In September 1960 box office takings had been giving concern – the weekly average amounted to £822 per week against a budgeted £909, and there was a total deficit of £3,800. Things improved, however, the following year with a record number of admissions of nearly 250,000 (which meant that the theatre average was 57 per cent of capacity, compared with a national average of under 30 per cent), despite an increase in seat prices, which of course also helped to lift the weekly receipts. This year also brought an objection from the Cinematograph Exhibitors' Association that the theatre was attempting to popularise its programmes – an objection which has reared its head from time to time since. The outstanding success of a retrospective season of notable Westerns may have accounted for this but otherwise, apart possibly from short spells of horror films, American thrillers and a look at Gary Cooper, it is difficult to see the justification for the complaint. Ten years ago, programmes on pre-*Blow Up* Antonioni, Visconti, Leopoldo Torre-Nilsson, Pabst and Murnau, and New Talent from the Argentine, can hardly have been considered pandering to the casual filmgoer. A series of three programmes on jazz ("Jumpin' at the NFT") consisted of films, extracts, tape recordings, photographs and live performances.

Highlights of 1962 were comprehensive Fritz Lang, Renoir and Vincente Minelli seasons, and a series of films shown for their propaganda and anarchist content. Original prints of two First World War films, *The Battle of the Somme* and *The Battle of Arras*, shown as part of a number of programmes on the period and provided by the Imperial War Museum, proved so popular that the museum was prevailed upon to loan them for three extra days. The NFT celebrated its first ten years by screening films which had received their first showing in this country at the theatre. They included:

    Les Amants (Louis Malle)
    Pather Panchali (Satyajit Ray)
    Les Quatre Cents Coups (Truffaut)
    Moderato Cantabile (Peter Brook)
    L'Avventura and *Il Grido* (Antonioni)
    Shadows (John Cassavetes)
    Ballad of a Soldier (Grigori Chukhrai)
    Ikiru (Kurosawa)

and formed an impressive indication of its pioneer work. There was also a Festival of Wild Life Films under the patronage of the Duke of Edinburgh, with lectures by Peter Scott, Bernard Grzimek and Armand Denis, and films ranging from Cherry Kearton to Walt Disney. 1962 closed with a Howard Hawks retrospective which carried on into the following year.

The 1963 season featured the British director David Lean, the American producer Sam Spiegel, the veteran King Vidor, and surveys of two Japanese masters (arranged by John Minchinton), Yasujiro Ozu and Kenji Mizoguchi. An interesting event was the survey entitled "School of Vienna": the work of film-makers in some way associated with the Austrian capital and its 'cult'. Erich von Stroheim, Fritz Lang, G. W. Pabst and Josef von Sternberg were all born in Vienna. Max Ophuls, though born in the Saar, has always been linked with the Vienna of popular imagination. Films from all these directors were featured in the season. A French programme, 'The Real Avant Garde', consisted of a number of silents which foreshadowed the type of film so described a few years later. It included episodes from the early Feuillade serials *Judex* and *Fantômas*, together with a complete performance of *Les Vampires* at one sitting – with a very necessary break for refreshments. The year closed with a brief Polish season.

Six critics, Ian Cameron, John Coleman, Dilys Powell, John Russell Taylor, Alexander Walker and Francis Wyndham, were given a choice of programmes during 1964 – asked to select six of their favourites without regard for what might be included in a 'Ten Best' list. An analysis of their preferences is interesting: out of 36 chosen, 21 were American, 3 Italian, 7 French, 1 Argentinian (Torre Nilsson's *Hand in the Trap*), and only 4 British. None was silent, only a few pre-World War Two, and about a third were thrillers. All the selections were screened at the NFT. By popular demand the complete *Les Vampires* of Feuillade was revived, and was booked solid four weeks beforehand. Encouraged by this success, the management followed it at a later date with similar full-length screenings of all the episodes of the same director's *Judex*, *The New Mission of Judex* and *Tih Minh*, each programme lasting some 6½ hours, with intervals for refreshment as before. The year included a special three-day collection of exchange programmes of Russian Cultural and Scientific Films, and a gala screening of *Intolerance* at the Odeon, Leicester Square, with a special score composed and played by Gerald Shaw on the cinema organ. The most controversial event, however, was the first part of a season on "The Thirties", which dealt with Germany and featured a number of films made under the Nazi regime and during the war, including the famous *Olympiade*, *1936* directed by Leni Riefenstahl, *Titanic*, and *Die Grosse Freiheit Nr. 7*.

At the end of April the South Bank building was closed in order that improvements and extensions could be put in hand, and for the next eight months the NFT programmes were shown at the Vickers Building on Millbank and the Shell Building. Both were comfortable and hospitable venues, but both – apart from the fact of not being 'home' – had drawbacks. There were no facilities for spoken commentaries, which meant that non-subtitled foreign films could not be shown, and the Shell Building safety regulations precluded the use of inflammable (i.e. pre-1952 nitrate) film. This was a serious drawback, because almost four-fifths of the cinema's history comes within the inflammable film period and many of the prints used by the NFT are on nitrate stock, awaiting the time and money to be copied. For this reason it was possible to show at the Shell only two films in the season "The Thirties, Britain" – two films which happened to have been already copied on safety stock. The auditoria in both cases were much smaller than at South Bank, Vickers holding some 200, Shell 300. And after all this effort, the extension and other plans had to be abandoned. The move had been made on the understanding that the NFT extension would be built, but owing to difficulties which arose between the LCC and the contractors, negotiations broke down and resulted in deadlock.

The re-opening of the theatre revealed an additional annoyance which was more disruptive than might at first be imagined. During the period of exile, a bridge expansion gap had been installed between the existing Waterloo Bridge and the new Waterloo Bridge Road approach. As a result, there can have been few visitors to the NFT around that time who have watched a quiet film (particularly during the early session) without the unwelcome accompaniment of an intrusive and infuriating clack-clack of cars and lorries passing over the gap in the road above their heads. The Council went to considerable expense to alleviate the situation, but it was not until the middle of 1970 that the noise was completely eliminated.

The financial position became critical. The move had caused a serious decline in membership, which did not pick up until late in

1965; the NFT was in receipt of no governmental support whatever; it could not (and cannot) advertise, other than by means of its excellent but expensive booklet, for fear of incurring the displeasure of the industry on whose good will it so largely depends; and altogether not even the most optimistic of prophets could have foretold the successful opening of NFT 2 six long years in the future. Certain minor improvements had been made to the South Bank building, notably by the installation of 70mm projection facilities, but all in all this was probably the NFT's darkest hour, and it says much for the courage and faith of its administrators that the year ahead contained plans for some of its most interesting programmes. These included a Swedish season which excluded Bergman almost entirely in favour of lesser known directors, in particular Mauritz Stiller and Alf Sjöberg; a second Critics' Choice series; a short Greek season; 'Films from the Danish Film Museum' featuring the work of Dreyer and Benjamin Christensen; a tribute to von Sternberg (from *The Salvation Hunters*, through his obsession with Marlene Dietrich to his last picture *The Saga of Anatahan*); two very successful specialist programmes (on English Music Halls and Railways), both destined to be repeated; and a nostalgic feast of Busby Berkeley musicals, for which both the dance director and his leading lady Ruby Keeler made personal appearances.

This last carried over into 1966 and saw the Theatre in more promising circumstances, with membership figures rising once more and correspondingly healthier business at the box office. A comprehensive Joseph Losey season included a rarity – the first relatively complete showing of his much mangled and infamously dubbed *Eve*, made in 1962. Renoir's French and American productions of the forties and fifties followed, and later on a number of lesser known works of the New Wave period in France. The Japanese director Kon Ichikawa was represented by fifteen of his films, and a brief 'Beauty in Horror' season included the seldom seen Lon Chaney *Phantom of the Opera*. The year ended on a more cheerful note than had been possible for some time, with the news that for the first time the Treasury had agreed to allow the Institute to make a small contribution from its grant to the theatre, and that the GLC (as the former LCC was now called) had approved the revised plans for an extension. Only four more years to wait!

The next year, 1967, opened with a somewhat depressing survey of the cinematic treatment (or maltreatment) of history – from such models of ruthless rewriting as Paul Czinner's *Catherine the Great* (with fey little Elisabeth Bergner as the formidable Empress and handsome American Douglas Fairbanks Jr as her mad boor of a husband), and Rowland Lee's libelling of Richard III in *Tower of London*, to the more serious and careful reconstructions and biographical portraits of Paul Muni's *Juarez* and *Pasteur*. The year also included studies of Marcel Carné and writer Jacques Prévert, and a Godard season from *Breathless* to *Made in USA*. A long Italian season filled the summer months, covering 1930–65 and a wide field of directors, known (De Sica, Visconti, Fellini, Rossellini) and comparatively unknown (Blasetti, Zampi, Lizzani, Zurlini): unfortunately the ambitious project was not a financial success. On the lighter side were programmes dealing with the work of W. C. Fields and Harry Langdon, and a special evening on the great period of the cinema organ, finishing up with Don Baker at the New York Paramount Theatre Wurlitzer playing 'Tiger Rag' blindfold, "using all four manuals and changing stops as he goes!" On Hallowe'en a special all-night Horror Programme was held in aid of the Italian People's Flood Appeal Fund. It lasted from 6.15 p.m. to 6 a.m. and included *Ghost Breakers*, *The Uninvited*, *The Cat and the Canary* and, according to the brochure, "a liberal stirring of Dracula, vampires and ectoplasmic extracts. At the midnight hour free toad and hemlock soup will be served". The ordeal proved so popular that all-night programmes later became a regular occasional feature.

To mark the fiftieth anniversary of the Russian Revolution a season was arranged, by David Robinson, under the general title *Ten Days that Shook the World*. In it a number of Russian films were grouped chronologically by content to present a continuous story of the Revolution and the years that followed. On two evenings a special programme was presented dramatising the story from the end of the nineteenth century to 17th October, 1917, through words, music, actors, speakers and film, using members of the National Theatre and directed by Lindsay Anderson who, with David Robinson, also wrote the scenario. Other specialist programmes include two lectures given by Richard Bebb on filmed opera (a third, built around Gian-Carlo Menotti's *The Medium*, followed early in 1968), and a visit by the world-famous tenor Giovanni Martinelli which had an unexpected side-effect of the highest importance for the NFT. (See the John Player Lectures, p. 125.)

In the middle of 1967 Richard Roud was succeeded as Programme Director by Peter John Dyer, at one time editor of the *Monthly Film Bulletin*. Plans for a conning-tower and staircase to act as a focal point indicating the new NFT entrance (now buried beneath the approach pathways around the Elizabeth Hall and the Hayward Gallery) were dropped in favour of a neon sign.

One of the most successful of all NFT seasons, the full-scale retrospective of the work of Buster Keaton, formed an auspicious start to 1968. The enormous popularity of this joyous occasion led to equally successful public showings at the Academy Theatre – to the NFT's considerable advantage – and to further revivals. It signified the belated recognition of Keaton as possibly the greatest comedian of the cinema. "If only," wrote John Gillett, "he could have been here with us." Keaton died in 1966 – but happily not before the start of his great revival. Arranged with the assistance of Raymond Rohauer, the season contained almost all his films of note – including a fine new print of the unsurpassed *Seven Chances* – and a comprehensive selection of shorts. *Seven Chances* had been shown previously during the 1965 London Film Festival in a print (the only one then known to be available) romantically saved from destruction but somewhat the worse for wear: even in this less than satisfactory condition it had caused laughter that must have penetrated through to the traffic passing on the bridge above the roof.

Another highlight was the entire output of Rouben Mamoulian – sixteen films – also arranged with Raymond Rohauer and introduced with great charm by the director. Notable were *Applause* and *City Streets* with their examples of early ingenuity in overcoming the new dimension of sound; *Dr Jekyll and Mr Hyde* with Fredric March (by far the most successful version and full of brilliant camera work); *Becky Sharp* with its use of colour for dramatic effect; *Silk Stockings*, a musical version of Lubitsch's *Ninotchka* (in which "Garbo laughed"); and Garbo herself in her most memorable role of *Queen Christina*. The Mamoulian season introduced a new element into NFT programmes – a three-way conversation between audience, interviewer and film-maker. Mamoulian came to England especially for the event and discussed his work with the audience after each show. This tradition has since been widely extended and is regarded as a very important aspect of the Theatre's purpose.

Billy Wilder and Alain Resnais were represented by seasons of their work, and there was a valuable Hollywood Twenties survey, with silent stars such as Clara Bow, Louise Brooks, Betty Bronson, Adolphe Menjou, Gloria Swanson, William S. Hart, Marion Davies and Valentino – affording opportunities rarely available to see not only the masterpieces but the 'routine' entertainment productions of the great period. It was during this season that one of the 35mm projectors caught fire during the running of a nitrate print. The film, dramatically appropriate, was *The Four Horsemen of the Apocalypse*. The machine itself was badly damaged, and the performance was cut short – but the theatre was in action again the following night when the programme fortunately called for the use of the 16mm projectors. Considering how many nitrate-period films are screened at the theatre, the fact that in twenty years only one has caught fire is a remarkable record, and an indication of the care which is taken in their use.

In the middle of the year – at the other extreme – was shown the largest selection of American Underground movies ("some good – some bad", to quote the brochure) yet assembled in Britain. About sixty works were screened – a foretaste of the 1970 flood. Directors included were Andy Warhol, Ron Rice, Harry Smith and his Magic Cinema, Bruce Connor and the West Coast School, Robert Breer, Peter Kubelka and Stan Brakhage. Tickets were 10s for nine and seven hour shows. Chief among the 'specials' was a 'Human Rights' season prepared by Brian Baxter and chosen to illuminate "man's strength in the face of whatever seeks to crush or subdue him." Films selected included Bresson's *Trial of Joan of Arc*, Buñuel's *Los Olvidados*, Hitchcock's *The Wrong Man*, Vidor's *Our Daily Bread*, Dreyer's *Ordet*, Losey's *King and Country*, Lang's

Fury, and the too little known *Reach For Glory*, directed by Philip Leacock from John Rae's novel *The Custard Boys*. In October a new experiment was tried out – the reservation of every Friday night for a series of films by a particular director. Playing safe, the series began with Hitchcock. It opened, as a sort of trailer, with four popular works, the first being *The Lady Vanishes*, but later reverted to chronological order and ran right through 1969 to end in January 1970 with his current picture *Topaz*.

The main event of 1968 was, of course, the inauguration of the John Player Lectures in October, considered in detail in the following chapter. From now on programmes were to some extent linked with the lecturer who would (it was hoped) appear at a given date. Thus seasons of films directed by George Cukor, Stanley Donen and Nicholas Ray, and written or produced by Carl Foreman, opened 1969. This was followed by a programme of Spectaculars, from the rare *Miracle of the Wolves* (1924) to Poland's remarkable *Knights of the Teutonic Order;* from Abel Gance's triple-screen epic *Napoleon* (1926) to the "Epic that never was", von Sternberg's *I, Claudius*.

An innovation was the BBC series of 'Golden Silents', in which Michael Bentine introduced bits and pieces from the famous comedies of Keaton, Langdon, Chaplin, Larry Semon, Laurel and Hardy, Charley Chase and others. The BBC filmed the programmes on the NFT stage with NFT audiences because they felt it was through the response of such audiences that the tradition of the great silent comedians had been maintained. Admission was free and the programmes were afterwards transmitted – for months, for years – on television, giving in their fragmented form little idea of the true subtlety of timing, build-up and conjunction of absurdities which make up the true art of the great silent comedian, and unhappily accompanied by recorded laughter which however genuine choked the spontaneous equivalent in the viewer's infuriated throat. The silence was not golden enough.

Another series, more conventional but more satisfying, was entitled 'Cornerstones', consisting of films which pioneered new departures in cinematic art, technique or taste, or which seemed especially representative of a particular *genre* or movement. The choice was catholic, ranging from *A Blonde in Love* to Pabst's

Westfront 1918, The Last Laugh to *The Grapes of Wrath, The Unknown Soldier* (directed by Edwin Laine and the first film from Finland ever shown commercially in this country) to Wyler's *Jezebel, Cat Ballou* to a second showing of Gance's *Napoleon*. A tribute to Columbia Pictures involved a selection from some 1,500 films: here again variety was the keynote, from Jean Harlow in *Platinum Blonde* to *Lawrence of Arabia, Mickey One* to *One Night of Love*.

During August and September the South Bank building was closed for several weeks on account of building work in connection with the second theatre. During the period the NFT ran the Keaton season at the Academy already referred to. Its run was interrupted for two personal appearances by Lillian Gish in a programme produced by Nathan Kroll, forming one of the Player Lecture series and linked with screening of *The Birth of a Nation*. Admission to both lecture and film was open to the public, with priority booking for BFI members. The return to the South Bank was marked by a programme on 'Revolution in the Cinema' – outstanding films revolutionary in nature or content – a complete season of Samuel Fuller's work, and a tribute to the veteran Hollywood producer Hal Wallis, comprising eighteen of his hundreds of productions. All-night shows included gangster films, a 'Horror Homage' to the late Boris Karloff, and the model 'Dynamation' work of Ray Harryhausen from such films as *Jason and the Argonauts* and *Mighty Joe Young*. Specialist programmes during the year included two Australian films never shown before in Britain and introduced by Bruce Beresford of the Film Production Board, and the ever popular Railway films, presented by John Huntley. Responsibility for programme planning was taken over by Ken Wlaschin.

On 7th February 1970 the NFT, with membership recruitment in mind, reopened its doors to the public in Saturdays, but *not* with continuous performances. Prices and booking were as for other days, and the films shown were mainly modern classics already commercially released but not often available elsewhere. The year's programmes began with a season of 'Swashbucklers' (Errol Flynn, Douglas Fairbanks Snr) carried over from the close of 1969, 'The Evolution of the Musical', and a tribute to Noël

VISITORS TO THE NFT

(*above*) James Cagney, with James Quinn, 1957. (*top right*) Fellini giving an informal talk, 1960. (*centre right*) King Vidor, during the "First World War" season, 1962. (*bottom*) Jean Renoir examining a presentation made to him on the occasion of his visit during a retrospective season of his films in 1962. Left of him, Leslie Hardcastle; right, Richard Roud

Rouben Mamoulian with Miss Jennie Lee, during a season of the
former's films, 1968
Judy Garland with her husband, Mickey Dean, 1969.
(*right*) Francois Truffaut, director of *L'Enfant Sauvage*, which opened the
fourteenth London Film Festival, 1970

Coward linked to his Player Lecture. In order to meet many requests for seasons devoted to particular actors a series of all-night programmes was inaugurated, starting on 14th February with Will Hay, followed by Humphrey Bogart, W. C. Fields, Peter Lorre, Vincent Price, John Wayne and others. Main seasons included the Japanese Kurosawa, Brazilian, Polish and Israeli cinema, and the controversial 'Film and Nazi Germany' series already referred to. Friday evenings were devoted to Bergman. A number of animated film evenings were arranged, including an all-UPA cartoon festival and a number of Lotte Reiniger's beautiful silhouette films. Following this was a major season devoted to Walt Disney – a rare opportunity to study his work in concentrated and roughly chronological form. The season was an unexpected success, especially with younger audiences, many of whom were discovering a new world in cinema for the first time. A Roger Corman tribute consisted mainly of his well-known Poe horror stories, but included also a few less familiar non-horror items from his vast output, together with the premiere of his account of the Ma Barker gang of the thirties, *Bloody Mama*, in its uncut version. A chance to see the complete works of Robert Bresson, arranged by Brian Baxter, was a rare delight for those who find in his austere, uncompromising, restrained work – as Baxter does – some of the greatest poetry in the history of the cinema.

The Cinema City Exhibition cast its shadow before in a programme of over fifty features tracing the History of the Cinema and intended as a prelude to its opening. During and after its run the NFT screened a series based on its construction, with divisions into Great Performances, Comedy, Epic, Fantasy, Thriller, Musical, Romantic and Western. The accent was on the classics, ancient and modern, but included also were a few films familiar by title but rarely seen in Britain for many years, such as *Old Ironsides* and *The Love Parade*.

In the middle of all this interesting but reasonably conventional activity was held the world's first international underground film festival – running from Monday 14th September and finishing with an Underground Forum on the following Sunday, at which leading film-makers had been invited to take part. Sharing in this

H

venture were the London Film Co-op, the New Arts Lab, the Oxford Film Co-op and The Other Cinema. More than 500 films were shown, day and night, in nearly 100 hours of viewing. The cost to the NFT and the John Player Fund was around £600: some 5,000 people were estimated to have attended the screenings, which were mostly free. Sample titles: *Hot Leatherette, How to Screw the CIA, The Absolute Elsewhere, "Adolf Winkelmann Kassel 9.12.67.11.54h", Heinrich Viel, Yoghurt Subculture, ½-Open and Lumpy, Sketch on Abigail's Belly, Boobs a Lot, Robert Having his Nipple Pierced.* One aim of the festival was to break down the gap between the general film-going public and the Underground enthusiasts and directors. The extent of the success of this laudable objective cannot yet be estimated, but it is doubtful whether the Forum was very much help. Any attempt by anxious inquirers to discover what the Underground movement meant was resolutely resisted. "Why should the underground mean anything?" was one remark. "Why can't we let the footage run?" In the theatre foyer a large notice read: "No smoking, not even pot." All in all it was, as Leslie Hardcastle commented, "quite an experience".

The major event of the year was, of course, the opening of NFT 2, after years of frustrating and abortive endeavour. When he took over as Chairman, Sir William Coldstream had made this project of a second theatre a major personal concern, and it was largely owing to his perseverance and determination that on Monday, 21st September 1970, the doors were opened. The idea behind the 165-seater cinema, forming part of a £125,000 extension scheme, is, in the words of its programme planner, Brian Baxter, "to help fill the gaps that one medium-sized cinema must leave." For all its modest size and compactness, NFT 2 has full facilities for screening films of any period, silent or sound, and any size from 8mm to 35mm, together with provisions for earphone commentary. In this respect, in fact, it has the edge over its larger brother in that it includes a five-way language translation system which will enable it to be used for foreign language lectures and conferences as well as for films. Closed circuit television and large-screen television presentations can be arranged at short notice.

Programming, designedly flexible, has been based on a rough "day-a-week" season framework: Wednesday nights for Archive films, Thursday for documentaries, Friday for the specialist, etc. The theatre opened with a four-day premier of the second feature film to be sponsored by the Film Production Board, *Loving Memory*, directed by Tony Scott. Finance was provided jointly by the Board and by Memorial Enterprises. The film, the first to be made by its young director, was also the first to win the Vivien Leigh Award.*

Shorts and silent films are planned to form a greater proportion of the screenings than is the case at NFT 1; a Silent Film Festival, arranged with the help of Anthony Slide, editor of "The Silent Picture", was, in fact, the first full-scale season to be held in the new theatre, running concurrently with, and complementary to, the Fourteenth London Film Festival.

In addition to the large-scale seasons and specialities surveyed above, the National Film Theatre is in use throughout every year for one- or two-day events such as the Newsfilm Award Festivals, films by students of the London Film School (formerly the London School of Film Technique), the Short Film Makers, the British Industrial Film Festivals, sponsored films presented by the Federation of Film Societies, Arts Council programmes on Art and Artists, to name but a few. There are also numerous formal occasions. Very few 'big names' in the world of the cinema have not visited the theatre at some time or other. Queen Elizabeth II, Prince Philip, Princess Margaret and other members of the Royal Family attend special performances on particular subjects (e.g. Wild Life), diplomats and officials from foreign embassies, members of the Government (and the Opposition) pay visits in official or unofficial capacity. But the NFT exists, and recognises that it exists, first and last for the *filmgoer* – the lover of movies – whether student, teacher, esoteric enthusiast,

* On 10th September, 1968 an Anglo-American Gala performance of *Gone With the Wind* was held in the presence of Prince Richard of Gloucester and the American Ambassador, David K. E. Bruce. The proceeds went into a special fund called the Vivien Leigh Award, to be donated by the Production Board to a specific film which has some particular quality, associated with an outstanding performance by an actress – in this case Rosamund Greenwood.

historian, professional critic, or simply plain (and no less important) fan.

Policy and planning

The basic NFT policy is simple – to offer as many filmgoers as possible as many opportunities as possible of seeing as many films as possible in as good conditions as possible. Stating a policy is one thing. Planning and carrying it out is another. The NFT caters for a present membership, mostly young, of some 45,000 people who love movies, and since 1952 it has shown some 50,000 features. During the course of a year it will be possible, with the new theatre in operation, to see some 700 full-length films every year. "The problems of organising such an activity," Leslie Hardcastle admits, "are sometimes a little frightening. The things that can happen during a Chinese season, or to the rare colour print of Douglas Fairbanks Snr's *The Black Pirate*, which requires six hours' servicing every time it is projected, are best not thought about. . . . And which other cinema requires its projection staff to understand Lithuanian or Arabic, its box-office staff to pronounce Ugetsu Monogatari correctly or its manager sometimes to cope with sixteen changes of programme a week?"

And all this has to be done, as we have seen, on a largely self-supporting basis, at least until three years ago when the BFI grant was permitted, though even this is only as a safeguard against loss – a deficit grant.

"The NFT," says Hardcastle, "runs a cultural activity in a commercial way. Sometimes we are accused of being *too* commercial, but the plain truth is that we have only money enough to be experimental for a short period at a time. In any case, what is 'commercial' and what is 'experimental'? Chaplin was never looked on as a great artist in the early days – in fact he was the most 'commercial' film-maker of his time."

A rough break-up of the annual film programmes given by Ken Wlaschin, Head of Programme Planning for NFT 1, shows that 35–45 per cent come from distributors in Great Britain, 15–20 per cent from the Archives in Britain or abroad, and the rest from foreign producers – the latter generally for a special season on some particular director or country. Films obtained from distributors in this country are provided free of charge – the theatre could not function otherwise.* For this reason alone is its obviously necessary that a good relationship should always be maintained between the NFT and the industry. "Distributors are on the whole extremely co-operative," Wlaschin says, "often going to considerable trouble to supply us with the titles we ask for. On our part we try to help them as much as we can. For instance, a good house for a certain film originally released some years ago and then put out of circulation, might be an indication to the trade that there is a public waiting to see it, and that it might be worth while considering a reissue." This is particularly the case in the present revival of interest in 'old' films – a revival which undoubtedly had its origins in the success of such programmes at the NFT, as well as in television broadcasts. It must be remembered, too, that as a general rule a film will be shown for one night only at the theatre, which negates any competition with commercial interests. For Saturday performances, to which the general public are admitted, a special fee is arranged; the films for these programmes have to be selected from those in commercial distribution because of the necessity of their having received certification from the British Board of Film Censors. "The whole arrangement is not an ideal one: demands on certain sections of the industry, notably the distributors of Continental films, may sometimes be felt to be unduly high. Nor is it entirely satisfactory to the Institute: to beg for daily favours, even from good friends, can be irksome, and it is a tribute to the patience of the trade that the system has worked so well for so long."†

Even with this co-operation, financial considerations impose severe restrictions on the choice of films. The cost of bringing one 35mm film by air mail from Japan, for instance, may amount to £160. If it is without subtitles, the necessity of providing a

* A decision has been made recently to pay a modest service fee universally applied to all distributors to safeguard the essential supply of films, and particularly to relieve the pressures on those small specialist distributors who, by the nature of the product they handle, supply the majority of the films the NFT require.

† *Outlook, 1965.*

translation and commentary may add another £85 or £90 to the bill. This means that, in order to break even, it will be necessary to screen two or more films from local sources in order to pay for the single Japanese print. These restrictions will, of course, operate even more harshly in the case of NFT 2. "It is impossible for us to make a profit," says Brian Baxter, "and therefore we just cannot expect to be able to show many imported films."

With several hundred films a year to book (and it may take several weeks of work to secure one film for one showing on one night only), programmes have to be planned in general outline approximately twelve months in advance, and in detail some five to six months. As a result bookings will sometimes have to be left unconfirmed or even cancelled at short notice, with consequent disappointment to visitors. The one complaint above all others laid against the NFT is the poor quality of some of the prints. Members may turn up, possibly from long distances, to be met with a notice saying that the only copy available of the film advertised has turned out to be a blown-up 16mm of dubious quality: or worse still he may, without warning, be shown a mutilated, scratched, jerky travesty. If he does not know what the much-lauded masterpiece looked like in its original form he receives a totally false impression of its quality, and wonders what all the fuss was about. If he *does* know, he is likely to become an even deeper shade of enraged purple as he realises the injustice done to a great piece of cinema. The NFT is only too aware of the situation, but, as Leslie Hardcastle says, "it is hard to find a correct answer. For example, the only copy of *Intolerance* at present available in Britain is a 16mm one. Should we show this, with all its shortcomings, or borrow a beautiful 35mm tinted print from New York? Obviously, the latter. But (a) the cost of bringing such a film from America, by air mail, is very high indeed, and (b) they wouldn't in any case loan it to us very often. We are as concerned as anyone. Sometimes the projectionist will ring up the office in a state of the greatest excitement – 'Come and look! Come and look!' – and we will run to the theatre to find that we have an old and rare print in first-class condition. It's a great moment for all of us – when it happens."

Ideally every film should be viewed before it is shown to an audience. In that case it would at least be possible for an announcement to be made from the stage explaining the circumstances, pointing out the shortcomings of the film to be seen, and the parts, if any, that are missing, and declaring that, frankly, it was 'this or nothing'.

When Chaney's *The Hunchback of Notre Dame* was screened a few years ago the entire central episode of Quasimodo's whipping and receiving comfort from Esmeralda – a key sequence and essential to proper understanding of the plot – was missing entirely. In the 1932 version of *Dr Jekyll and Mr Hyde* on one occasion a number of short cuts had destroyed some of the most effective moments in the film. These are just two random instances when a few words of explanation would, to a small extent, have mollified many a savage breast. Unhappily, shortage of time and staff make this procedure impossible at present, and, as Hardcastle points out, even if it were possible for someone to view the film, in many cases he could only judge the quality of what was there, and would not realise how much was missing unless he knew the original. Still, it is obviously desirable that some sort of explanation should be given when goods are delivered in short measure.

In the actual methods of presentation the NFT has consistently maintained praiseworthily high standards, governed by a respect for its product which might well set an example to many commercial cinemas. The dreary, cheapening, 'grinding-on-regardless' continuous performance; the tedious, seemingly endless intervals for advertisements (which may well keep away more money in admission tickets than they bring in from the advertisers); the tray-cluttered salesgirls marching down the aisles during the final moments of the film (or even in the middle of it) to their spotlit stands beside the screen – these deterrents against filmgoing do not sully the NFT.* "Our aim," says Hardcastle, "is to show the best of world cinema, past, present and future, under ideal technical conditions, to bring film-maker and filmgoer together both by showing the former's work and by personal discussions."

* A British exhibitor visiting America recently wrote in a trade paper (with intent to disparage) "Sales of ice cream in the auditorium was a rare service." To which one can only reply "would it were so elsewhere".

Above all, the NFT is to be commended on its approach to the problem of the foreign language film and the question of dubbing. * This abominable practice has practically nothing to be said in its favour. As Sir Alec Guinness has said, "to lose an actor's voice is to lose half his performance." Apart from this, however skilfully the matching is done, it is always noticeable, and always destroys all illusion of reality. The mere knowledge that a lot of foreign actors and actresses are suddenly speaking perfect English is sufficient to break any spell. Indeed, it sometimes leads to sheer absurdity, as when, in a recent vast epic, Russian soldiers after talking broad Cockney suddenly burst into song in their own language. The unhappily increasing use of this monstrosity in commercial cinemas (with honourable exceptions) seems to be due to a supposition that cinemagoers find it preferable to subtitles. This is highly questionable. As in the case of many 'popular' programmes on television, it is probable that many people go to see a dubbed foreign film because it is the only version offered to them. In a recent viewing session for Film Societies a dubbed version of Alain Jessua's *Jeu de Massacre* was turned down by a majority of 11-6, with such comments as "Not dubbed, sorry", "Ugh, dubbed!", "No good dubbed", "Ruined by American dubbing, the original is much funnier." A suburban cinema manager is telephoned by intending patrons, when a foreign language film is being shown, who want to be assured that a subtitled – not a dubbed – version is being used, before they visit it. The furore caused by the dubbed version of *Les Demoiselles de Rochefort* a year or two ago caused its withdrawal and substitution by a subtitled one – "now you can see it as it *really* is!" It is a ludicrous procedure to antagonise the discriminating filmgoer in order to make what is probably a mistaken attempt to placate the casual – who will very likely choose another film for his evening's entertainment whichever method has been used.

This monstrous hybrid is resolutely rejected by the NFT, who

* Confusion is sometimes caused by indiscriminate use of the word 'dub' when 'post-synchronise' would be more accurate, e.g. when an actor re-speaks his own words in a recording studio. 'Dubbing,' where speech is concerned, is best reserved for occasions when the words do not, and are not intended to, synchronise in literal fact, i.e. when an actor attempts to fit the words of one language on to the lip movements of another.

will only in the case of direst necessity show a dubbed film. In the case of *Rififi*, for instance, one of the most significant films of its period, only one print is known to exist, and that a dubbed one: it was a case of that, or nothing – and after consultation it was decided to screen it. (It is worth remembering that the famous climax of *Rififi* is a 20-minute robbery sequence in which not a word is spoken.) For foreign films which have not been subtitled the NFT employs a commentary spoken in English, formerly over loudspeakers but now through individual earphones so that each member of the audience can please himself whether or not he takes advantage of it. These commentaries are prepared with the utmost care whenever time allows. Not every word is translated: a precis is made of the main speeches, and only the essential parts rendered into English. Whenever possible a professional actor will be engaged – someone who 'knows when to breathe'. The commentary is spoken in a quiet, informative voice, with *no acting*, no emotional content. This is absolutely essential. The object is to inform, not to rival the actor who is playing the part on the screen. Should a film arrive at the last moment without subtitles it is sometimes necessary, for want of an available actor, to engage an international simultaneous interpreter, but this is not so satisfactory. He is apt to spell out every word and, as Hardcastle puts it, 'he breathes all the time'.

It may well be that some variation on the NFT commentary method will emerge as the best method of dealing with the foreign language film. Earphones or speakers are probably impracticable for general use, but there have already been instances of a sort of voice-over commentary, spoken in a manner similar to that at the NFT, which is superimposed on the existing sound-track, with very acceptable results.* Clearly, whatever method is adopted, the result will be a compromise. All the present systems have their drawbacks. Subtitles can spoil the image to some extent, particularly in dark sequences; they are often difficult to read against white backgrounds, though it is possible now to outline the letters in black; they are sometimes badly printed, broken and jerky, full of misprints, and badly

* For example in a short Polish film known here by its French title *Au Feu, Au Feu, enfin il se passe quelque chose*, directed by Marek Piwowski.

translated. The claim that they are distracting, however, is much exaggerated. The knack of reading them is acquired within a few moments of the film's beginning, and thereafter, providing the subtitling is well done (as it generally is nowadays) the sense of the spoken words is assimilated almost unconsciously. (The subtitling of films shown on BBC television is an example of how well the job can be done and with how little distraction to the viewer, even when the lettering has to be a considerable height from the bottom of the frame.)

Commentaries also have their drawbacks, particularly when the wearing of not very comfortable earphones is involved.

When, however, there are several alternatives, however imperfect they all might be it seems a lunatic proceeding deliberately to choose the worst. There must be many people who have had their first introduction to subtitles or English commentary through joining the NFT, and thus discovered how relatively painless a way either of them is of enjoying the true flavour of a foreign film. For its part in spreading this knowledge, and its resistance to the canker of dubbing, the NFT deserves the gratitude of every enlightened filmgoer.*

The audience

In 1968 the NFT sent out a questionnaire entitled "Who are those people, sitting in the dark?", designed to complete a survey of its audience, "their tastes and habits – where they come from, what they do for a living, how old they are, how often they go to the National Film Theatre." The form was sent to 1,500 full members and 3,000 associates, and there were 1,185 replies. The method

* A variation on the dubbing of a foreign film which would be better described as post-synchronising is to be found in cases where the majority of parts are played by, say English-speaking actors with some foreign ones, generally small parts, who say their lines as best they can in English, and these lines are afterwards matched up by other English or American players. This is done often when on location in other countries, and also when matching singers' voices to actors' faces in musicals – and occasionally when an actor, too late for substitution, proves vocally inadequate. This is true synchronisation and if discreetly done frequently passes undetected and is acceptable. What is never acceptable, and what is referred to above, is slapping the words of one language on to the lips of another and hoping one will not notice. One always does.

was, admittedly, rough and ready. The very fact that 26 per cent
had troubled to fill in their questionnaires at once classified them
from the rest. Nevertheless the breakdown is worth noting, divided
first into occupations:

	FULL MEMBERS		ASSOCIATES	
	Male	Female	Male	Female
	%		%	
Business	24.0	26.8	33.5	42.2
Professional	26.3	1.8	26.9	5.7
Student	7.3	3.6	10.2	10.9
Lecturer / teacher	10.6	19.6	8.3	10.4
Journalist / writer	5.8	7.1	2.4	1.14
Civil Servant / Local Government	6.7	5.4	11.5	10.4
Librarian	1.4	12.5	0.8	2.6
Entertainment	14.5	10.7	5.4	4.7
Retired	0.83	—	0.5	2.08
Housewife	—	8.9	—	7.3

Of these, the majority – a clear 48.5 per cent, were in the 23–24
age group. Twenty-nine per cent belonged in the 35–50 group;
less than 10 per cent were older than 50. The remaining 13 per
cent were between 16 and 22. Two out of three lived in a London
postal district, three out of four worked in a London postal
district. On the whole, full members were the most regular
attendants. The greatest number, around 20 per cent of the total,
said they averaged one visit a month, but many more full members than associates said they attended upwards of fifteen times a
year. About 8 per cent of male full members (considerably less of
associates and females) attended weekly.

The most noticeable change in the $2\frac{1}{2}$ years since the survey is
the lowering of the majority age group from 23–24 to 16-22, due
largely to the increasing study of film in universities and colleges.
"Four years ago," Hardcastle says, "the type of audience used to
change with the type of film – to some extent you could tell what
type of programme you were showing by looking at the audience
instead of the screen. Now the difference is not so marked. There
are still plenty of older people – some of them probably making a

sentimental journey to see once again a favourite silent or early sound feature – but in the main it is now a young audience and, for the first time, an audience to whom television and cinema is their own language. In the last eighteen months, too, a new element has grown up. We have always had occasional protests, but now almost everything we do may be seized on as an excuse for some protest or other. When we had a Brazilian programme, a 'pressure group' persuaded Brazilian film-makers to withdraw half their films because the Brazilian Government was carrying out an unpopular policy. The position is often unpredictable. It was perhaps understandable that a Nazi programme should be attacked by the British Council of Jews, but when we put on an Israeli season and thought we might get blown up by the Arabs – and took precautions against this – we found instead that we were offending the left-wing Israelis."

Even the Walt Disney season gave offence to certain people of unusual political sensitivity (or inordinate love of protesting) who professed to find racist trends and effete capitalistic propaganda in the activities of Bambi, Dumbo, Goofy, Snow White and the rest, and raised their dutiful voices in condemnation. Donald Duck's response to such grave charges would, one feels, have been brief, but worth hearing.

Despite the enthusiasm, informed interest, and general love of the cinema to be found in the majority of NFT audiences, they contain (if the dictum is correct that inability to appreciate the thought and work of ages other than one's own is a sign of mental immaturity), at least their fair share of cretins. The giggles, titters and generally puerile behaviour of a would-be sophisticated-seeming minority became so prevalent a few years ago that it was actually found necessary to put up notices in the foyer requesting them to show a reasonable standard of consideration for others and, whatever their private opinions (if any) at least not to ruin the pleasure of their neighbours. In the autumn 1968 issue of the magazine *Film* Kevin Brownlow attacked them vigorously in an article entitled 'When the Tittering has to Stop'. Whether the films were in themselves good or bad examples of their period made little difference. The fact that certain manners and conventions were not those of their own little day was enough for the gigglers – the thorns crackled under their pots at the masterpiece and the mediocre irrespectively. In recent years the position seems to have improved – perhaps the titterers have now reached Coronation Street age and are staying at home – though their place has to a smaller extent been taken by chronic protesters. There is no doubt, however, that the mindlessness of the few can affect the pleasure of the many, with consequent loss at the box office. This is one problem with which the NFT certainly should not have to contend.

2. THE JOHN PLAYER LECTURES

One day in 1967 Leslie Hardcastle encountered a gentleman wandering in rather lost fashion along the corridors of 81 Dean Street. He said he was looking for the offices of the National Film Theatre, and that he was interested in giving away quite a lot of money. Understandably, Hardcastle received this statement politely but with some slight reserve. However, he invited the visitor into his room and they had a talk – the outcome of which was a visit to the NFT. Leslie Hardcastle still had no idea of the stranger's identity, or what concern, if any, he represented. It happened that the programme on this particular evening at the cinema was a specialised one on Opera and the Film, featuring a talk by the famous tenor, Martinelli, and the visitor was very much impressed.

In actual fact, the arrival of the mysterious stranger was not quite as casual as it seemed to be, and Stanley Reed, the Director, had already been made aware that a major sponsor was interested in the Institute's activities. Not long after Leslie Hardcastle's brief encounter the John Player Lecture Series was set up, one of the Institute's most unqualified successes, despite the fiasco of its opening session. The firm of John Player has long been noted for its generous interest in sporting and artistic operations. Following their representative's recommendation, they informed the BFI that they would be prepared to support the National Film Theatre in some special project, and asked for suggestions. As a result, a number of schemes were put forward, one of which was a series of lectures. Celebrity lectures and personal appearances have, of course, been held at the NFT since its inception, but these had been occasional affairs and without any overriding plan. Now, however, the opportunity had arrived to provide for a definite series of talks by the most celebrated people connected with the film world – directors, actors and actresses, producers, technicians – and it was seized with both hands. The grant for the first year was £4,800, for which Players required twelve lectures – twenty-four were given. For the following year the grant was £7,650 and a total of twenty-four suggested – forty-eight were given. The third year started in October 1970, with the same grant as the previous year and plans for an even more ambitious season. In addition to the regular series, John Player Lectures are scheduled for a number of regional film theatres, including Newcastle, Manchester, Brighton and Nottingham; a new series entitled 'Aspects of Cinema' at NFT 2 will open with four illustrated talks by Richard Williams on the art and history of animation, to be followed by technicians, musicians, educationalists and others discussing their work; and a final important development will be the inauguration of the 'John Player Annual Lectures', in which a leading academic figure or film-maker will deliver three formal lectures (a characteristic of the regular Player Lectures is their informality) on a subject of his own choosing. It is hoped that these Annual Lectures will subsequently be published. If plans go ahead as hoped, all these projects will have become realities by the time this book appears.

Apart from the requirement of a minimum number of lectures, John Player & Sons allow the theatre an absolutely free hand, making no stipulation, for instance, about advertising, though it has now been agreed that the series should officially be known by the name (which they have in fact been given all along) of the John Player Lectures. At first the lectures were held at 2.30 on Sunday afternoons, and full members of the Institute were allowed free tickets. This led to some abuse, however, as many members accepted their tickets and then did not use them. As a result, people were being turned away while 20 per cent of the seats remained empty but reserved. In June 1969 the time was altered to a later hour, and as this meant the cancellation of the first film show a charge was made for all admissions.

To open the important first series the French director Jean-Luc Godard had been invited, and had accepted. Realising that he was dealing with an elusive person, Leslie Hardcastle went personally to France, and spent two days chasing him around Paris "in a James Bond fashion". Eventually he managed to run him to earth and present him with an air ticket to London. Godard grabbed the ticket, ran away down the corridor of the building, opened a cupboard door in mistake for the way out and was showered by the contents, dashed on to the street, and was whisked away in a car. On the day of the Lecture a packed house, including television and film cameramen and sound recordists crowded in the aisles, waited for the arrival of the master. And waited. Eventually, Leslie Hardcastle walked on the forestage with a telegram in his hand. Somehow, nobody was very surprised, though a good many were more than a little mystified by its contents when they were read out. "If I'm not there take anyone in the street, the poorest if possible, give him my £100* and talk with him of images and sound and you will learn from him much more than from me because it is the poor people who are really inventing the language. Your anonymous Godard." On this cryptic – if not meaningless – effusion a note in the NFT booklet commented, with generous restraint, "M. Godard failed to turn up, but sent the above telegram which tells more about the man than at first appears." In certainly suggested the extent of his regard for the audience to whom his films are presumably addressed, many of whom had come long distances to hear him, and for the theatre which had done him so much honour through the years and to whom he owed much of the respect he (strangely, some think) commanded in this country. "We shall continue to show his films," Leslie Hardcastle said generously, and the talk was replaced by a screening of one of them. But many of the audience felt they had had enough for one day, and went home.

The failure of this beginning was quickly dispelled by the success of the second lecture, when Richard Lester gave a brilliant and penetrating analysis of the position and the problems facing

---

* There was no specific £100. Lecturers are paid expenses but not, unless in special circumstances, a fixed fee.

the present-day film-maker. Bad luck, rather than deliberate dis-
courtesy, hit the third lecture, when Fred Zinnemann was taken ill,
but George Axelrod, writer, producer and director, took his place
and drew a witty, amusing and somewhat caustic picture of the
American film world. A month later Jacques Tati more than
compensated for his compatriot by enchanting a full house for 1½
hours with "arguably the finest one-man mime-comedy act seen
on a British stage this decade." Perhaps one did not garner much
grave knowledge of his methods of work, but the whole distillation
of his films seemed to be there in person, and it is doubtful
whether the Waterloo Bridge arch had rung to such continuous
laughter since the showing of Keaton's *Seven Chances* at
the London Film Festival a year or two before. Eventually the
wholly captivating M. Tati had to be gently, and with the
utmost regret, escorted from the auditorium ("I would have
gone on for another half-hour," he said) because the 4 p.m.
audience would be kept waiting no longer – for *La Guerre est
(Finie)*.

Since then the series has proceeded with imposing success. A
complete list of the speakers who have appeared up to the winter
of 1970 is given at the end of this book, but apart from the individual lectures Open Forums have been held on a wide variety of
subjects, at which producers, directors, stars, critics and others
connected with the art and industry of the cinema have partici-
pated in free discussions. Among those who have taken part are
Richard Attenborough, Bryan Forbes, Jack Gold, John Halas,
Ken Hughes, Ken Loach, Carl Foreman, Gerald Thomas, Donovan Winter, Charles Cooper, Charlton Heston, Leonard Whiting,
Nina Hibbin, Margaret Hinxman, Derek Malcolm, Philip Oakes,
Dilys Powell, David Robinson, John Russell Taylor and Alexander Walker.

Even though speakers receive no fixed fee, travel and accommodation expenses can be considerable. The admission price
barely covers the cost of staffing the theatre, so that the budgeting
of the series is entirely dependent on the John Player grant, plus
a small fee paid by the BBC for television rights to certain
lectures which is paid into the fund to enable additional ones to
be held. To cover each event a small but comprehensive booklet

Lillian Gish, 1968

Jacques Tati, 1968

Graham Greene, 1969

Billy Wilder, 1969

JOHN PLAYER LECTURERS

Alfred Hitchcock, talking to Bryan Forbes, 1969

is issued with biographical and other information about the speaker and his work.

Subjects are not limited to the actual making of films. Jack Valenti, President of the Motion Picture Association of America and former Special Assistant and Adviser to President Johnson, spoke on the practical concerns of the industry; Professor A. J. P. Taylor the historian, on the film and Nazi Germany; and Dr Christopher Evans, Principal Research Fellow in Computer Science at the National Physical Laboratory, on movies and dreams, and "dream movies". There is no shortage of willing lecturers. "In the early days," says Søren Fischer, John Player Lecturer Officer, we had to go out to find speakers. Now very often they, or their agents, will come to us. To date, since the opening lecture, no one we have approached has refused our invitation."

3. THE LONDON FILM FESTIVAL

From achieving a theatre of its own, it was a short step for the BFI to consider holding a festival of its own. This was impracticable during the lease of the Telekinema building, which was really something in the nature of an experiment throughout, but through the enthusiastic efforts of James Quinn and Sylvester Gates, then Director and Chairman respectively, plans went ahead as the new theatre was being constructed, and the first London Film Festival inaugurated the new National Film Theatre. A strictly non-competitive event, this was launched by the BFI in association with the *Sunday Times*, who provided a guarantee against loss, and consisted of the most notable films seen at such international Festivals as Cannes, Berlin, Venice, Karlovy Vary and Edinburgh. It included Bergman's *The Seventh Seal*, Fellini's *Nights of Cabiria*, Torre Nilsson's *House of the Angel*, Clair's *Porte des Lilas*, Elia Kazan's *A Face in the Crowd* and Wajda's *Kanal*.* There was no British entry in the feature class, but one or two shorts were screened, produced by Pearl and Dean, Halas and Batchelor, and the London Transport Commission. The reason for this, which applies to all the London Festivals, is not necessarily

* A complete list of LFF feature films will be found in Appendix E.

an indication that there were no films from Britain of sufficient quality, but that release arrangements preclude their being shown beforehand.

As might be expected, each year's programme contains some films which are certain of subsequent commercial booking, others which will always remain in a specialised category, or even disappear altogether into some cold vault.

The early festivals consisted of a number of public performances and others reserved for BFI members. This arrangement is now slightly altered, in that the public is admitted to all performances, but members receive booking priority and lower seat prices.

The following year disagreements arose between the BFI and the *Sunday Times*, who wanted the Festival held in a West End cinema rather than the NFT. The *Sunday Times* bowed out, and subsequently the LFF was run in conjunction with the LCC, and later the GLC. Since its inception it has remained the highlight of the NFT year (despite formidable competition from time to time) and was, in fact, described by the BFI Chairman of Governors in 1967 as "the most important event in the Institute's Calendar." It has been responsible, for instance, for first intoducing to the United Kingdom the work of new and then unknown directors such as Olmi, Antonioni, Louis Malle and Milos Forman.

The 1958 programme contained another Bergman destined to become world famous, *Wild Strawberries*, John Sturges' *The Old Man of the Sea* (with Spencer Tracy), Jacques Baratier's *Goha* (with a handsome if somewhat raw young man called Omar Cheriff – later to achieve fame as Omar Sharif) and Louis Malle's *The Lovers*. Once again England was represented only by shorts. During this Festival an International Film Conference on Film Appreciation was held at the BFI's premises in Great Russell Street. The LFF is the high season for foreign visitors, and each year has its quota of directors whose films are represented.

On the closing night a new international film award was presented for the first time. It took the form of a sculpture in silver by Gerald Benney and was presented to the Institute by the Duke of Sutherland for an annual award to be made each autumn at the LFF. This was to go to the maker of the film from any country first shown at the Theatre during the preceding twelve months which, in the opinion of the Institute, had made the most powerful and beneficial impact on people in Britain seriously interested in the cinema – audience, critics and film-makers. The selection panel consisted of a committee of Institute officers, and critics, and the award was known as the Sutherland Trophy – now the British Film Institute Award. The first award went to Yasujiro Ozu's *Tokyo Story*, with a Special Mention to Jiri Trnka for *The Luchian War*. It might be convenient to list here the subsequent awards, which were:

1959	Satyajit Ray's *The World of Apu*
1960	Antonioni's *L'Avventura*
1961	Olmi's *Il Posto*
1962	Rivette's *Paris Nous Appartient*
1963	Resnais' *Muriel*
1964	Kozintsev's *Hamlet*
1965	Godard's *Pierrot Le Fou*
1966	André Delvaux' *The Man who had his Hair cut Short*
1967	Kobayashi's *Rebellion*
1968	Jean-Marie Straub's *The Chronicle of Anna Magdalena Bach*
1969	Rivette's *L'Amour Fou*
1970	Bertolucci's *The Conformist*

The third Festival, becoming perhaps somewhat over-ambitious, threatened to run into difficulties, partly because of the failure of a week of short and animated films to bring in sufficiently large audiences, and partly because of a very expensively produced brochure. The NFT has made numerous attempts to overcome the resistance to short films (of which there are many hundreds, a large proportion of them British, which never get the showings they deserve) and, as we have seen, it is part of the policy of NFT 2 to carry on and widen the campaign. Notable among the feature films were Camus' *Orfeu Negro*, Bergman's *So Close to Life*, Truffaut's *Quatre Cents Coups* and Buñuel's *Nazarin*. Also screened was the first feature-length film to be made by the United Nations Film Service, *Power Among Men*, produced and conceived by Thorold Dickinson and J. C. Sheers, directed by Alexander Hammid, G. L. Polidoro and V. R. Sarma. The film had won prizes at Berlin, Moscow and Venice. There was, in addition, a three-day Children's Films Festival.

Italy and France predominated in 1960, with several co-productions as well as individual pictures. Films shown included Chabrol's *Les Bonnes Femmes*, Truffaut's *Tirez sur le Pianiste*, Antonioni's *L'Avventura* and Visconti's *Rocco and his Brothers*. Jean Renoir's *La Règle du Jeu*, made in 1939, was shown as a special event – the first time the complete version had been seen in Britain. Peter Brook's French film *Moderato Cantabile* was also screened.

By this time the demand for festival seats was so heavy that there were widespread complaints from members about the impossibility of getting into the theatre – grievances which persist to this day. If the Festival is to retain its character as an event of the NFT, if the public are to continue to be admitted, if there are no more arches to build cinemas under, and no more money if the arches were there, it is difficult to think of a solution. Mainly this is on account of the trade restrictions: the International Film Producers' Association limits the London Film Festival to two weeks duration: the film producers and distributors, on the whole, fix a limit of two screenings per film. The problem *would* be solved if the two groups could be persuaded to allow the Festival to run longer and to permit additional screenings as was the case in the early years.

High spots of 1961 (fifth Festival) were Pasolini's *Accattone*, Olmi's *Il Posto*, Torre Nilsson's *Hand in the Trap*, Demy's *Lola* and Godard's *Une Femme est Une Femme*. The Festival made a profit of £734.

The year of the NFT's tenth anniversary, 1962, opened with Renoir's *The Vanishing Corporal* and included Buñuel's *The Exterminating Angel*, Polanski's *Knife in the Water*, Bresson's *Trial of Joan of Arc* and Godard's *Vivre Sa Vie*. By special arrangement with the producers, a British film was included – a midnight matinee of Tony Richardson's *The Loneliness of the Long Distance Runner*.

In 1963 the NFT had the satisfaction of knowing that the Lincoln Center for the Performing Arts, sponsors of the first New York Film Festival, were basing it on the London pattern. The seventh London Film Festival, in fact, was planned to run as a joint operation with the New York first. France and Italy were again dominant in the programmes: Olmi's *The Engagement*, Rondi's *Il Demonio*, Resnais' *Muriel*, the compilation film *Rogopag*, Malle's *Le Feu Follet*, Chris Marker's *Le Joli Mai*, and his short *La Jetée*. Occasionally a resurrected 'old-timer' has been included in festival programmes. This year it was the great French silent comedian Max Linder's three American features put together by his daughter under the collective title *En Compagnie de Max Linder* – a rare treat.

Owing to the abortive extension plans for the NFT the eighth Festival was held at the Odeon, Haymarket by courtesy of the Rank Corporation. This break with tradition, while altering the character of the occasion to some extent, had the advantage of enabling more people to gain admission to the programmes. Outstanding films included Demy's *La Baie des Anges* and *Les Parapluies de Cherbourg*, Godard's *Bande à Parte*, Buñuel's *Diary of a Chambermaid*, the Canadian *Nobody Waved Goodbye* (directed by Don Owen), and Pasolini's *Gospel According to Matthew*. The latter was shown on a Sunday morning at the large Odeon, Leicester Square and caused a sensation. Britain was, for once, strongly represented by two notable productions. The first was Kevin Brownlow's *It Happened Here*, a nightmarish vision of what life in England could have been like under a Nazi occupation – seven years in the making (the director was eighteen years old when he began it), and done on a budget which would have considered a shoestring a luxury. The Festival closed to a shattering finale with Losey's *King and Country*, preceded by Polanski's biting little short comedy *Mammals*.

By 1965 the success of the LFF was arousing such interest in the latest Continental productions that prize-winning films from foreign festivals were being bought up before the Institute could get the right to show them at its own festival. Consequently its nature began to some extent to change. For the first six or seven years of its existence it had lived up to its name as the festival of festivals, which took up all the prize-winners from all the other festivals, though it had for some time included in its programmes a number of productions which had not been officially shown elsewhere. Now, however, it increasingly found itself becoming a festival of unknown works, or works by unknown directors – still retaining its strictly non-competitive ruling.* These were referred to as London Festival Choices, and in the ninth Festival included the Swedish *Dear John*, directed by Lars Magnus Lindgren, and destined for wide distribution later. A 'London Retrospective' choice was Keaton's masterpiece, *Seven Chances*, one of the season's highlights. The prize-winners still predominated, however, and in fact still keep their majority, though with a lower percentage. Prominent among these in 1965 were Godard's *Alphaville* and *Pierrot le Fou*, Milos Forman's *A Blonde in Love*, James Ivory's *Shakespeare Wallah*, Franju's *Thomas L'Imposteur*, and Dreyer's *Gertrud* which encountered extremes of admiration and antipathy.

The following year's offerings were fairly evenly divided between first works by new directors, films by established names, and second or third films by directors not yet widely known in this country. They included René Allio's *The Shameless Old Lady*, memorable for a remarkable performance from the veteran French actress Sylvie, Torre Nilsson's nightmarish *The Eavesdropper* and Alexander Kluge's *Yesterday Girl*. Among London Choices were Godard's *Made in USA* and Alexandre Astruc's *La Longue Marche*. A smaller proportion than usual achieved wide distribution, and it was considered that, though a financial success, the tenth Festival's general standard of films showed a falling off. There was even a rumour that it might be the last. This was entirely unfounded, however, and the following year proved one of the most successful to date, including Bo Widerberg's *Elvira Madigan*, Bresson's incomparable *Mouchette*, Berkovic's *Rondo*, Skolimowski's *Le Départ*, Buñuel's *Simon of the Desert* and (a London Choice) Robbe-Grillet's *Trans-Europ Express*. Other London Choices were the American *Funnyman* (directed by John Korty), the two Russian Lenin films, *Heart of a Mother* and *A Mother's Devotion*, and the Yutkevitch Eisenstein reconstruction *Bezhin Meadow*.

The next year, 1968, was the Festival of Upheavals. Cannes was knocked out and Pesaro badly bruised by violent demonstrators

---

* In 1970, only seven out of the twenty-eight films shown had been purchased for UK distribution before the commencement of the Festival.

determined to wreck the proceedings for political motives on the principle, apparently, of what I don't like you can't have. This is not the place for a discussion on the pros and cons, but the sight of eminent directors squabbling and scuffling on the stage and the determination to use films as weapons for political bickering and reduce them to the levels of petty partisanship, did little credit to either cause or cinema. The silly brawling spilt over – in a very small way – on to the twelfth LFF, with the showing of Godard's first English-language feature film, *One Plus One*, a London Choice. Apparently without the director's approval, the producers, Michael Pearson and Iain Quarrier, had altered the ending. In an effort to be fair to both sides, the LFF ("proud to present" the film) decided to screen both versions. At the same time M. Godard had given a copy to some 300 students who were going to take over the theatre. "Halfway through the evening," Hardcastle recalls, "I had 500 people coming out of the first house, 500 going into the second house, 200 trying to buy tickets, and 300 students showing their copy on the pavement. In the middle of all this Godard was being introduced on the stage. The producer, Iain Quarrier, remarked that he would like to explain his side of the story, whereupon Godard, who had admittedly suffered a tiring and trying day with one press conference after another, ran across and hit him full in the face. Then the situation became a little difficult. Fortunately, outside at least, the British weather came to the rescue and it began to pour with rain." With *One Plus One* out of the way, the rest of the season seems to have been conducted on a more adult level, and there were a number of outstanding films: Jean-Marie Straub's *Chronicle of Anna Magdalena Bach*, Kjell Grede's *Hugo and Josefin*, Chabrol's *Les Biches*, Jan Troell's *Who Saw Him Die?*, among them. London Choices included Lindsay Anderson's *If . . .* , Harry Kumel's *Monsieur Hawarden* and Bergman's masterly – and to date little seen – *Shame*. The season as a whole was notable for the presence of directors whose work had been shown at previous festivals from their very first films.

An increase in London Festival Choices was noticeable also in 1969. Partly, as *Sight and Sound* pointed out, this may have been due to the luck of London's timing, able to draw on the new late-autumn film crop, but it was also perhaps a reflection on the general festival standard of the year. Berlin and Moscow offerings in particular were considered below par. The outstanding success among the London Choices was Ken Loach's *Kes*, and the selection also included Claude Guillemot's *La Trêve* and Marguerite Duras' *Destroy, She Says*. Among the prize-winners were Bresson's first colour film *A Gentle Creature*, Eric Rohmer's *My Night with Maud*, and two from Japan, *Double Suicide* (Shinoda) and *Boy* (Oshima). 1969 was Richard Roud's last as Programme Director. He was succeeded for the fourteenth Festival by Ken Wlaschin.

France came up strongly in 1970 with three masterpieces from established directors: Truffaut's *L'Enfant Sauvage*, Chabrol's *Le Boucher* and Franju's *La Faute de L'Abbé Mouret*. Bergman was represented by his first documentary, the subject of which was *The Island of Fårö*, used as the setting of many of his recent fiction films. From Japan came Kurosawa's first film in five years (and his first ever in colour) *Dodeska-den*, and Yoshida's *Eros + Massacre*; from Poland, Wajda's *Landscape After Battle;* from the US, Barbara Loden's *Wanda;* from Italy, Liliana Cavini's modern version of Antigone, *The Cannibals*, all helped to make up formidable competition with previous years. An unexpected success was *The Night of Counting the Years*, from the United Arab Republic. Britain was represented by *Bartleby* (directed by Anthony Friedmann), with memorable performances from Paul Scofield and John McEnery. In his introductory note Ken Wlaschin drew attention to the unusual number of exceptional acting performances, and this was especially true on the feminine side – Stéphane Audran in *Le Boucher*, Jane Asher in *Deep End*, Gillian Hills in *La Faute de l'Abbé Mouret*, Britt Ekland in *The Cannibals* and Stéfania Sandrelli in *The Conformist* all helped to make the fourteenth Festival notable, and to remind the pundits that it is not only directors who 'make' films.

Simultaneously with, and complementary to, the LFF of 1970 a two-week Silent Film Festival was run at NFT 2, arranged by Brian Baxter and Anthony Slide, editor of *The Silent Picture*. The season featured a number of very rarely available silents of particular interest just because they were *not* among the permanent and much screened masterpieces. The list included Raoul Walsh's *The Wanderer*, with Greta Nissen; Clarence Badger's *She's a Sheik*, with Bebe Daniels; Charles Brabin's *The Whip;* William Beaudine's *Heart to Heart;* Charles Hines' *Brown Derby;* and a Ken Maynard Western, *California Mail.* Better known titles were Borzage's *Seventh Heaven;* Marshall Neilan's *Daddy Long legs*, with Mary Pickford; Raoul Walsh's *What Price Glory?* and Herbert Brenon's *Beau Geste.*

On the financial aspect of the London Film Festivals, Leslie Hardcastle says; "Each year we take a gamble, spending so much money in advance, and hoping it will come back at the box office. Each year rising costs have to be taken into account. For 1970 we had to spend an extra £1,000 simply to keep up with the previous year's expenses. The GLC contribution for 1970 was £1,250, a figure which has remained unchanged for some ten years, and there is also a contribution of £400 to £500 from the film industry. We are limited to our 500 NFT seats because even if a larger commercial cinema was available the exhibitors and distributors would not approve of our using it, and we depend to a large extent on their co-operation. For the same reason our performances of any particular film are limited to two, perhaps even to one screening. In spite of these limitations we just about pay out way. In 1969 we lost £1,000: in 1968 there was a profit of £300. Over the years, the LFF probably breaks even."

4. THE PIANIST

No account of the National Film Theatre could claim to be complete without mention of Arthur Dulay, who has accompanied its silent films on the piano since its inception at the Telekinema.

While he was studying at the Guildhall School of Music, Arthur Dulay acquired a reputation as a technician with a rich gift of extemporisation. Hearing that money was to be made, in a small way to start with, as a cinema pianist, he applied for such a job, was forbidden by the college authorities to play professionally, disobeyed, and – in accordance with the (as he admits) very reasonable rules – had his scholarship cancelled.

"I always seemed to be able to fit my playing to the mood of any picture," he says, "to tell a story with my fingers at the piano – and above all that's what I love to do." His first job was at an 'electric palace' opposite the present Windmill Theatre, known as Pyke's Circuit – a site still occupied by a cinema, but now showing a somewhat different category of film. Here he started as "relief pianist", at an upright instrument with a knob at either end which converted it when required into an organ. It also enabled both to be played together, "making a devil of a row". Later he became a member of a fourteen-piece orchestra at the West End Cinema (now the Rialto), Coventry Street, sometimes filling in as relief also, and playing up to 4½ hours at a stretch.

With the coming of sound Dulay, in common with many another cinema musician, felt the pinch. For some years he worked in an office in Wardour Street in a clerical capacity, but eventually he managed to break into broadcasting. He formed his own quintet, and his own 'cameo orchestra' specialising in the popular classics, working also as accompanist and as 'general utility man'.

"If they wanted an effect in a play of someone practising scales, or playing the piano when he was drunk, or something of that sort, they would come to me."

In 1952 the conductor John Hollingsworth asked him if he would like to play for the old silent films once again. Dulay treated the suggestion as a joke, but when he learned it was serious he accepted with alacrity – found himself at the Tele-kinema, and has played for the National Film Theatre ever since.

Dulay rarely makes use of existing music in his film accompaniments unless what is happening on the screen suggests some known work to the audience: everything else grows from his own imagination as he watches the picture. And he seldom needs to run a film through before accompanying it at the NFT. "I've seen them all already," he says.

About five years ago, returning home from the theatre in a hired car, he was involved in a bad road accident. For a fortnight he was in hospital, and afterwards had to undergo treatment and therapy. "During all this time," he says, "the Institute treated me with the utmost kindness." He had suffered no serious internal injuries nor felt a great deal of pain, and at first it seemed that he would escape lightly, but the accident led to the development of Parkinson's disease, as a result of which he cannot now walk at all without assistance. However, though he has three deputies, Florence de Jong, Robin Saunders and Philip Coleman, to relieve him, he still plays regularly at the NFT, and it is both moving and inspiring to watch this seemingly frail and helpless man being helped to the piano in a wheel-chair and then to hear him, when the lights have gone down and the old silent film starts to unfold on the screen, playing as he must have played fifty years before. NOTE: As this book reached its final proof stages, news came of the death of Arthur Dulay on the 18th June 1971. An obituary notice sent out by the Institute said, with truth; "His contribution to the success and growth of the National Film Theatre has been very important and he will be greatly missed by both the audience and staff."

5. THE REGIONAL FILM THEATRES

In its early days the British Film Institute had close connections with the provinces through the interest of local film societies, many of which became affiliated and took the title of British Film Institute Societies. After the war, following the publication of the Radcliffe Report and the establishment of the NFT, these links were weakened, and eventually the Institute was incurring criticism for becoming too tied to London in its activities. As early as 1955 Denis Forman had written: "Although the [National Film] Theatre is a boon to the London film-lover its value to other centres of population is of course negligible."* Seven years later, in 1962, a booklet celebrating the tenth anniversary of the NFT stated: "Among the other shortcomings of which the Institute is conscious is its almost complete failure to extend the work of the National Film Theatre outside London. Some people object, and with reason, to the use of the words *National* and *British* for what are in effect London operations. The Institute has every sympathy with the feelings of film-lovers outside London whose appetite is whetted, but never satisfied, with each appearance of the National Film Theatre programme booklets. For this problem there seems

* *The Film and the Public.*

no ready-made solution, for while it is just possible for the NFT to survive in London without major subsidy, this could not happen in less thickly populated areas."

Fortunately a solution – though perhaps not a ready-made one – began to appear three years later when, with the encouragement of Miss Jennie Lee, who was particularly interested in the dissemination of the arts throughout the country and in dispelling the myth of the intellectual superiority of the capital, the Governors of the Institute commissioned a report on the prospects for regional development which was published under the title "Outside London". This recommended that "the Institute should seek to establish centres throughout the country for the showing and study of films, on the lines of the National Film Theatre in London." Following on this, Stanley Reed, as Director, approached local authorities to seek support for the art of the film such as had already been given (with the aid of the Arts Council) to music, literature and drama. Plans were prepared, and in 1967 the first theatre opened. The Bristol Arts Centre was the pioneer organisation to sign an agreement to become a regional film theatre. Norwich was the first to open its doors to the public and Nottingham followed a few days later. The movement grew until, as this book is written, thirty-six regional film theatres are in active existence, of which three are full-time (Manchester, Newcastle – or Tyneside – and Brighton) and one (Newcastle) has twin auditoria. Many are on a one-week-per-month basis; some show films on one or two days a week. Two theatres are run directly by the BFI (Newcastle and Brighton), the rest have followed the recommendations of the original Governors' report that the Institute should "seek to stimulate action locally or regionally rather than undertake developments itself". Applications for further openings are dealt with as they reach the Institute. Those already founded have shown an interesting general spread across the country, and an equally interesting spread between the larger and smaller centres. Basildon and Belfast, Dartington and Edinburgh, Nottingham and Petworth are linked together with a common interest in and enthusiasm for the art of the cinema.

Local authorities are empowered to raise up to 6d (2½ np) on the rates for the purpose of subsidising the arts. They, or some other permanent source, are asked for a guarantee, averaging between £500 and £1,500, to support a regional film theatre. This amount, however, has by no means always been called upon in full, and may not even be needed at all. Generous support has also been forthcoming from various regional arts associations, led by the Northern Arts Association, supported by the Arts Council, local business and individual donors. The Department of Education and Science allocates an annual commitment and expenditure ration for regional film theatres, and such capital grants, as well as limited guarantee against loss, have to be matched by grants from local areas. There is also, in some cases, a revenue earned by the theatres themselves from outside hiring. Finally, of course, there is the revenue from the sale of tickets at performances, and from membership subscriptions, which are the financial mainstay of all the operations.

All theatres, with the exception of Bristol, hold both private and public performances – the former generally consisting of minority interest or uncensored films. Members receive priority treatment in advance bookings, and are sent a brochure of programmes and news items. In Newcastle one of the twin houses is reserved for members only. Anybody joining one regional theatre automatically becomes a member of all the others, and also of the NFT.

Theatres have been housed in public libraries, civic halls, university buildings, youth or education centres, commercial cinemas – anywhere, in fact, which is both available and suitable (see the list at the end of this chapter). New buildings specially designed have not often been able to achieve because of restricted funds and high costs, but there is no doubt that this would be the ideal. A new building will attract – and might even retain – a new audience, and where local authorities have risked the expenditure (as in Hull and Basildon) the result has been fully justified.

Films are selected locally, but in close liaison with the BFI. At one time the Regions thought in terms of modelling their programmes on those that had proved successful at the NFT, but it later became clear that local audiences preferred to decide for themselves what they wanted to see, and which classics were worthy of revival. Each theatre has its own committee, and, having made a selection of titles, they consult with Barrie Wood, Programme Planner for Regional Film Theatres (and previously Secretary of the British Federation of Film Societies), who advises them on matters of sales policy. This can be a complicated matter, because a regional theatre may wish to book a film for a single day whereas the distributor will only consider a two, six or even fourteen day period, dependent on the demand for, and date of, the film in question. This is frequently the case where foreign productions are concerned because of the small number of prints held. At present Wood is trying out a new method whereby regional theatres will allow certain dates every year to be pro- grammed and booked centrally: this would mean that (a) package advertising, programme notes, publicity and stills supply arrange- ments could be made, thus saving time, money and unnecessary duplication, and (b) recent films could get a quicker showing out of London. Most importantly, however, it might result in the breaking down of the six-day sales policy which is so frustrating for the smaller theatres, as it would probably be possible, on the one booking, to squeeze in a one or two day booking in one place and then send the film on elsewhere. As far as possible, and bearing in mind the restricted screen times in many cases, a series of films is shown in the context of a particular director, country or theme. These have often been as adventurous in nature as any at the NFT itself. In November 1970, for instance, a comprehensive season of the work of the Swedish director Bo Widerberg was arranged at Brighton, for the first time in this country. Films included *Love '65*, *Raven's End*, *The Pram*, *Elvira Madigan*, *White Sport* and *Adalen '31*. All except *White Sport* were open to the general public. A six-week Buster Keaton season was presented at the same Theatre during the summer of 1970, screened at correct silent speeds and accompanied by a team of four pianists on a rota basis. The success of this has encouraged plans for Keaton Festivals throughout the regions, starting with Newcastle in the spring of 1971. At Newcastle, as part of a season of films about revolution, a multi-media show on the same theatre was given, presented by Cy Grant and Herb Greer, and comprising songs, music, sound effects, poems, a light show, films and effects 'of all kinds'. Late night screenings are put on at Brighton every Saturday, and also

at Newcastle (Tyneside), where an all-night Underground programme has also been shown.

A survey taken in March 1970 by the small and fairly isolated
Aldeburgh RFT revealed that the highest attendance figures come
from the 20–30 age group (30 per cent); with the under-twenties
and 30–50 groups equal at 26 per cent each. The under-twenties
were the largest section (over 50 per cent) for a Sunday night
showing of a popular film (*Topaz*), but the smallest for a more
serious Saturday film, *Oh! What a Lovely War!* Those who
attended the cinema for films of relatively minority appeal came
fairly regularly (average 3 to 4 films a month) – about 80 per cent
of the population in the area practically never visited the cinema
at all. A report from Leatherhead showed 100 per cent attendances
for *The Whisperers* (with Edith Evans and Bryan Forbes present),
In the Heat of the Night, *Accident* and *Un Homme et Une Femme*
(each with one performance); and, with two performances each,
a top of 84 per cent capacity for *Elvira Madigan* and a bottom of
23 per cent for *Hugs and Kisses*. Pasolini's *Gospel According to
Matthew* achieved 82 per cent. Average attendance throughout
the first year of operations was the high figure of 78 per cent. A
special note from Aldeburgh expressed the general preference for
fixed times of performance.

As we have noted, plans are in hand for an extension of the
John Player Lectures to the regions, and though this may not be
without its difficulties (instead of mute, acquiescent cans of film,
important and often very busy people will have to be persuaded
to travel about the country), even a small measure of success
would justify the attempt.

A major scheme, which may set a pattern for similar under-
takings throughout the regions, was put into operation in 1970 on
Tyneside, where the film theatre is attended over the two main
academic terms by some 30,000 young people between the ages
of thirteen and sixteen drawn from schools. Known as the North
East Educational Film Project, and financed jointly by the Department of Education and Science and the Gulbenkian Foundation,
its plan is to combine film with education in a much wider range
than is possible under classroom conditions. Subjects include
twentieth-century history, art, education, careers, English litera-

ture, conservation, religious education, etc., at O-level and A-level standards. Short films, extracts, full-length features and documentaries are shown at both cinemas from 10 a.m. until 4 p.m. Smaller-scale but similar educational programmes have been arranged for Bolton, Bradford, Brighton, Bristol, Colchester, Corsham, Exeter, Hull, Leatherhead, Manchester, Middlesbrough, Newport, Norwich, Nottingham, Petworth, Sheffield and York.

At the close of 1970 the following Regional Film Theatres were in active operation:

Aldeburgh: 400 seats. The Theatre is closely associated with Benjamin Britten and Peter Pears, and runs a special programme during the annual Aldeburgh Festival. It was opened with a screening of *The Grapes of Wrath.* During the 1969–70 period a collection of comedy films was shown .

Basildon: 476 seats. An arts centre in a New Town. Opened by Lord Goodman, with *Never Strike a Woman Except with a Daisy.*

Belfast: 252 seats. Independent university film theatre in Northern Ireland. Opening film, *Viva Maria.*

Bolton: 300 seats. At the Little Theatre. Opening film, *La Trêve.*

Bradford: 299 seats. At the Bradford Civic Playhouse.

Brighton: 453 seats. A directly operated full-time theatre. Before the present theatre was set up, a trial venture took place at the Continentale Cinema (240 seats) in collaboration with the manager and backed by a small financial guarantee from the County Borough. The present theatre was opened by Richard Attenborough, who screened an advance clip from his *Oh! What a Lovely War.* The official opening film was *Elvira Madigan.* In addition to the seasons mentioned above, a six-week festival of Garbo films was shown during 1969. Celebrity appearances with their own films have been made by Kenneth More, Dame Flora Robson, Jack Warner, Sir Ralph Richardson, Tony Palmer, Jack Gold, Terence Morgan, Dame Edith Evans, and Shirley Knight. Towards the end of 1970 the Theatre held a gala performance of *The Birth of a Nation* to raise funds for refurbishing the building. This meant that, together with proceeds from a new seat-naming

Noël Coward, with Merle Oberon, arriving to give his talk. The theatre was filled with theatrical and other celebrities gathered to salute the occasion, 1969

James Mason, 1970

Dirk Bogarde, 1970

John Player Lecturers

Mervyn Leroy, being presented with a memento by the Institute's Director Stanley Reed, 1970

Richard Attenborough, with Dilys Powell, 1971

JOHN PLAYER LECTURERS

Regional Film Theatre contrasts – Aldeburgh

Regional Film Theatre contrasts – York

Regional Film Theatres – Brighton

scheme for the same purpose, £2,000 could be spent on re-seating and re-carpeting – a form of self-help which the Institute is anxious to encourage.

Bristol: 123 seats. Part of the Bristol Arts Centre. The first regional theatre to become operative. Opened by Lord Goodman, with *A Blonde in Love.*

Canterbury: 300 seats. A university film theatre. Opened by Lord Brabourne, with *La Femme Infidèle.*

Colchester: 319 seats. A commercial cinema presenting NFT programmes one week a month. Opened by Kevin Brownlow and Sebastian Shaw, with *It Happened Here.*

Corsham: 180 seats. A commercial cinema presenting NFT programmes. Opened by Stanley Reed, with *Elvira Madigan.* It also serves schools, the Bath College of Art and the Bath Festival. Its inauguration was hailed (by the film trade press) as an example of courage in opening a rural district cinema against a background of countryside closures.

Croydon: 1,500 seats. At the Fairfield Hall.

Dartington: 208 seats. An art centre. Opening film *Hugs and Kisses.*

Edinburgh: 110 seats. Located in the cinema of the Edinburgh Film Guild. Opened by Susana Ciganova, with *Romance for a Trumpet.*

Exeter: 433 seats. A university film theatre. Opened by Harold Pinter, with *Accident.*

Hull: 253 seats. A public library film theatre. Opening film, *Hugs and Kisses.*

King's Lynn: 366 seats. At the Guildhall. Opened by Lady Fermoy and Sir William Coldstream, with *Hugo and Josefin.*

Leatherhead: 526 seats. At the Thorndike Theatre. Opened by Dame Edith Evans and Bryan Forbes, with *The Whisperers.*

Leeds: 500 seats. At the Leeds Playhouse. Opened by Harold Lloyd with his film (unseen in this country for over thirty years) *The Kid Brother.*

Luton: 250 seats. A public library film theatre. Opened by Sir William Coldstream, with *Playtime.*

Malvern: 783 seats. At the Malvern Festival Theatre. Opening film, *Shakespeare Wallah.*

K

Manchester: 371 seats. A full-time independently run theatre. Opened by Sir William Coldstream, with *La Kermesse Héroique.*

Middlesbrough: 494 seats. At the Little Theatre. Opening film, *The Mistress.*

Newcastle (Tyneside): 592 seats. Directly operated full-time theatre with twin auditoria. Opened by Jonas Cornell and Agneta Ekmanner, with *Hugs and Kisses.* In addition to the season referred to above, a major Pop Festival was held in October 1969 to form part of the Newcastle Festival. Educational visits have been paid to the Theatre by Edward Short and Jennie Lee.

Newport: 400 seats. At the Little Theatre. Opened by Mrs Eirene White, with the Russian film of *Hamlet.*

Norwich: 772 seats. Combined university and town film theatre. Opening film, *Le Bonheur.* Visited by Joseph Losey.

Nottingham: 450 seats. At the Co-operative Educational Centre. Opening film, *Shakespeare Wallah.* As a contribution to the 1969 Nottingham Festival, the Theatre presented a season of Greta Garbo's films.

Petworth: 200 seats. Country project presenting weekly programmes for children and adults.

Prestatyn: 334 seats. A council-owned cinema presenting NFT programmes. Opening film, *Charlie Bubbles.*

Reading: 400 seats. A university film theatre. Opened by Mai Zetterling, with *The Girls.*

St Albans: 978 seats. At the Civic Centre. Opening film, *Fahrenheit 451.* Initiative for a regional theatre came from the Film Society, when a member of the committee asked if this were possible. The planning committee consists of representatives of the city council, the BFI and the St Albans Film Society – this three-part panel selects the films for each season.

St Austell: 200 seats. At the Arts Centre. Opening film, *Chimes at Midnight.* The theatre has been visited by Miss Jennie Lee.

Sheffield: 264 seats. A public library film theatre. Opening film, *Alone on the Pacific.*

Southampton: 500 seats. At the theatre of the College of Technology. Opening film, *Evergreen.*

Southend: 1,000 seats. At the Cliffs Pavilion. Opened by Irene Handl, with *Playtime.*

Street: 400 seats. At the Strode Theatre. Opening film, *Accident.*
York: 650 seats. A university film theatre. Opened by Gabriel
Axel and the Earl of Harewood, with *The Red Mantle.*

Seasons held at the various regional theatres have included
Swedish Cinema, French Cinema, British Cinema, Claude
Chabrol, Aspects of Violence, Danish Cinema, Shakespeare on
Film, The Jazz Age, Rod Steiger and the Actor's Cinema, Ameri-
can Underground, Play into Film, Polish New Wave, The
Permissive Society, Tribute to Losey, Japanese Cinema, Tribute
to Ealing, Andy Warhol Season, Fantasy and Horror, Pop Film
Festival, Buster Keaton Season, The Greatest Garbos, Federico
Fellini Season, Spectaculars, Revolutionary Cinema. There are
also regular specialist programmes, such as The World of
Cousteau, Birth of Film, The Creations of Georges Méliès, Music
Hall, Railways and the Cinema, The Industrial Revolution, The
Iron North, The Twenties, The Enchanted Isles.

From time to time complaints are voiced that the Institute
should "stop wasting its money" on the regions and concentrate
on developments in London: needless to say, it is from London
that such remarks generally originate. More constructive than the
I'm-all-right-Jack attitude were the words from Lord Eccles,
Paymaster-General and Minister for the Arts in the newly elected
Conservative Government: "In the field of the arts it is the job of
the Arts Council to select and fortify the highest standards and of
the British Film Institute to do the same for the cinema. But the
procedure holds good for improving the environment, for industrial conditions and for teaching moral and aesthetic values. The
quality of life demands that we should support that which enhances
the individual's understanding of himself and his society, and
which arouses in him the desire and the capacity to use his own
powers to the full. We know that in favourable circumstances art
can do this, but we shall not get very far unless industry and
education are working on the same plans as those who are responsible for the arts. For the first time the mass of the people are
asking for a share in life of a quality that satisfies the expectations
aroused by better education and the defeat of poverty. They are
determined to know themselves as individual men and women

not submerged in crowds manipulated from some distant head-quarters.

"To advance towards a society in which the quality of life is as important as economic growth calls for a new social strategy. So politics must change, and Governments go beyond the satisfaction of material needs and show an increasing concern for the imagination and spirit of all members of the community."

5

Production

The history of the BFI Production Board is divided into two parts, with an interval of some two years when it lay moribund for lack of funds. The idea originally grew from the Institute's association with the Festival of Britain in 1951, when it was responsible for producing stereo and other film novelties to be shown at the Telekinema. From this developed a plan to set up a permanent fund to subsidise promising young film directors anxious to embark on their first productions but lacking the money or sponsors to enable them to do so. Under the guiding hands of Denis Forman, then Director of the BFI, and Stanley Reed, the Secretary, a committee was formed with Sir Michael Balcon as Chairman – a post he has held ever since – and numbering among its members Howard Thomas, Sir Arthur Elton and Basil Wright. Preliminary meetings were held at Sir Michael's Ealing studios. There the Experimental Film Fund, as it was called, was launched – and there, as Sir Michael puts it, it stuck. Though under the patronage of the BFI the fund received no money whatever directly from it, and had to hunt for its finances elsewhere. Eventually, in 1952, it managed to get under way with a grant of £12,500 from the Eady Levy. This was a fund established voluntarily by the film industry in 1950 (it became statutory seven years later), created by a tax on cinema seats and designed to help British film-makers, in particular independent producers. Thus the Experimental Film Fund in its early days was entirely independent of the Institute and had no responsibility to its Governors – Sir Michael himself was not at that time on the Board. By 1958 the grant had been spent, on a total of fifteen completed pictures, and the committee was financing such productions as it could afford out of the distribution returns on its earlier films. In 1960 it received a donation of £10,000 from the Gulbenkian Foundation and this, together with its own earnings, enabled it to carry on, achieving a total production figure of some fifty films, for a few more years. To have accomplished even this much on the money available (described by Sir Michael as the cost equivalent of a couple of dud scripts on a spike) was something of a feat, but by 1963 its cash was finally exhausted, and it lay quietly down and turned its face to the wall.

For nearly two years it remained quiescent, but with the advent of Miss Jennie Lee as Minister of Arts, and as a result of the efforts of Stanley Reed who, as we have seen, made the fund's revival one of his first objects on becoming Director, the position improved, and for the first time the fund was allotted an annual grant in the budget of the Institute. This was only (for the first year) a very modest £5,000, but on 9th April 1965, the Committee held its twenty-sixth meeting after an interval of over eighteen months since the twenty-fifth. Most of its members now were people actively engaged in film-making, such as Edgar Anstey, Carl Foreman, Bryan Forbes, Karel Reisz and Basil Wright, but it also included two art critics, John Berger and David Sylvester, the theatre director William Gaskill, and Walter Lucas of the British Drama League, who were invited to join with the intention of broadening the range of interest. At the same time the fund's name was changed to the Film Institute Production Board, by which it is now known, because it was felt that the word 'experimental' could lead to "misunderstanding and acrimony. 'What's so experimental about *that?*' a critic may irritably ask, feeling himself thwarted of avant-garde delights. In fact, 'experimental' in this context was never intended to mean avant-garde."* It was, as a matter of fact, never very clearly defined.

The following year the grant from the BFI was raised to £13,000, and since 1966 it has remained at an average of about £10,000 p.a. "From now on," says Sir Michael Balcon, "as we were using Institute funds, we came quite properly under the control of the Governors – of which by this time I was one myself – and had to render an account of our stewardship. But

* *Outlook, 1967.*

our policy is still the same – a policy of freedom, which is not negotiable."

With this moderate security the Board was able to engage a full-time Production Officer, and took over part of the Institute premises at Lower Marsh, near Waterloo Station, which was stocked with equipment of excellent quality for the use of successful applicants.

The position of Production Officer has been held since its inception by Bruce Beresford,* who arrived in this country from Australia after directing films there and in Nigeria. Every script brought to the Board by an aspiring producer/director is read first by him. He then forwards it with a written comment to a member of the committee or to the Institute Director, Stanley Reed. After not fewer than three people have read the script it will, if considered suitable, be put on a short list which will then be sent to a full committee, who by this time will all have received a copy in advance. A large Board is maintained in order that, with many members possibly away at any one time working on films, etc., there will always be sufficient to form a quorum. The applicant will then be interviewed, and if he has previously made any films – or parts of films – will be invited to show them. Should an interesting script lack any supporting footage, and should there be uncertainty as to what decision to make on it, the BFI will pay for a test sequence. Members will, if necessary, go to see the material privately, or may write in detail to an applicant if it is considered this might be helpful. "We realise," states Sir Michael, "that (a) we are using public money, and (b) that what we are doing may affect the lives and careers of young people, and we take the job very seriously."

The Board's final approval gained, a budget will be allotted, based on the estimated needs of the script – "as low as possible," says Bruce Beresford, "but one which will allow the film-maker to make the film he wants." No actual cash is handed over, but the producer sends all bills to the BFI for payment. This is considered best for both parties, as with little or no experience as to how to go about getting what he wants the producer is apt to incur overcharging and unnecessary expenditure. He has free use

* See page 182

of all the Lower Marsh facilities for shooting, editing, projecting, etc., and though most of the work is done on location, modest sets can be erected if desired. These will often be made in conjunction with the Royal College of Art, who allow the use of their small studio. The producer is generally his own director, script writer, editor and photographer, but should he wish to employ any technicians the Board has an arrangement with the ACTT whereby they do not insist on union rates unless the film is eventually put out for commercial showings. In this case an adjustment is made. Another much appreciated concession is a grant of film stock made yearly by the Kodak Company.

Literally anybody can apply for finance. Many who do so are students or members of schools such as the London Film School. A number are foreign students living in this country. "Our main job is to bridge the gap between a young man's (or woman's) training at the National Film School when it starts, or any of the present teaching schools, and his first professional job in the feature field," Sir Michael Balcon states. "If you are to succeed in the entertainment world you need more on your plate than diplomas and degrees even if (as in the case of the Royal College of Art film section) these have university status. In addition the Board also enables people who have something to say to make a personal statement, even if they are not interested in the commercial theatre, *provided they can discipline themselves to learn how to communicate.*" The Film Production Board is still the only official source to which aspiring film-makers can turn for material and moral support.

Once the film is completed it may go through the commercial channels and earn money this way, but though the extra revenue is always welcome, this is not the object of the exercise. In fact, some of the films most successful commercially have been those thought least satisfactory by the terms of the mandate. Nevertheless, obviously the wider the distribution the better for both film-maker and Board, and any production will be placed as favourably as possible, particularly as any money brought in does not have to go back to the BFI but can be divided between the Board and the producer. FPB films have been shown at such cinemas as the Curzon and the Academy in London, many are sold abroad, and the Board now has an agency in America concentrating on the campus trade. Foreign television in particular is a good customer, and films have been taken by America, Canada, Germany, Australia and the Scandinavian countries. (Only three have as yet appeared on the television screens of its own country.)

Sometimes a film will be a slow starter, only to pick up rapidly later on. When *The Park*, directed by Richard Saunders, was completed in 1967 no one wanted to know about it, but during 1970 it was sold to three television stations. Partly to keep these possible channels open only comparatively few of the Board's productions find their way into the Institute's Distribution Library.

If only for financial reasons, the output is at present limited almost entirely to short films. The BFI receives between 1,500 and 2,000 applications a year, and has to deal with them on a budget which, as Bruce Beresford puts it, "might make two television commercials if you were careful." By vigilant costing and selection of scripts the Board manages to stretch its finances over some fifteen films a year with a running time of about twenty minutes each on average. For each of the two feature films completed to date, the Institute has gone into partnership. The first, *Herostratus* (1967) was financed jointly by the Board, the BBC and James Quinn, Director of the BFI during what might be called the teenage years of the Experimental Film Fund. *Herostratus* has been the Board's most ambitious undertaking so far. It runs 2 hours 20 minutes, is in colour, and cost £12,500. Its director, Don Levy, was already known to the Board for his work on shorts, notably *Time Is*, made for the Nuffield Foundation in 1964. *Herostratus* was launched with full commercial publicity coverage but, undoubtedly a minority film, never achieved general commercial release. It ran for some weeks at the Institute of Contemporary Arts in London, and subsequently at the Paris-Pullman cinema, the Arts, Cambridge, and elsewhere, and has had a fairly wide showing abroad.

The second feature, *Loving Memory*, and the Vivien Leigh Award of which it was the first winner, are referred to in the section on NFT 2 (see page 115). A third, *Jack Pudding*, by Richard

Saunders, overran its budget, and at the time of writing is held up for lack of money to put on the sound-track.

As may be expected, the Board comes in for its share of criticism – mainly on its choice of subjects. In any concern where many call themselves but only few can be chosen, a large residue of disappointment – and resentment – is bound to accumulate: as Sir Michael puts it, "Those we accept love us, the others – very naturally – don't like us so much." It would obviously be impossible for detailed reasons to be published for each rejection and each acceptance, and Bruce Beresford has set out his own general principles: "I don't believe that any type of film-maker is intrinsically better than any other. Some people try to convince me that left-wing films are necessarily valuable as works of art, or films about the poor in the East End, or about various downtrodden minorities. These subjects can all make good films, just as good films can be made about pop groups, but the really important thing is individuality – of viewpoint, of expression. The artist is the man who observes things for himself and, in his work, makes us experience the world through his eyes."* Many of the criticisms, in fact, tend to cancel themselves out. "Too experimental – not experimental enough: should concentrate on shorts – should become more ambitious and make features". It is worth remembering that in the case of both features so far completed extra finance was provided from outside the Board. The list of completed films also includes a number on which the Board came in with aid after the project had already been started.

Whatever its imperfections, there is no doubt whatever of the importance of the work the FPB is doing. During its first lease of life it helped directors such as Ken Russell, Karel Reisz, Tony Richardson and Jack Gold on the road to feature films. In its later lists are names, generally unknown at present, with every likelihood of becoming as successful as those mentioned above. Its first fifteen included three films (*Together*, directed by Lorenza Mazzetti and Denis Horne, *Momma Don't Allow*, by Karel Reisz and Tony Richardson, and *Nice Time*, by Claude Goretta and Alain Tanner) which were Free Cinema Productions; cartoons of varying styles; several art films (*Rowlandson's England*, *The Vision*

* *Time Out*, November 1970.

of William Blake, Coventry Cathedral); the Brussels prizewinner about children's games, *One Potato, Two Potato*, directed by Leslie Daiken; and Ken Russell's childhood fantasy *Amelia and the Angel*. A number of these won prizes at various festivals, and more recent winners have included *The Peaches* (Michael Gill, 1964), *Last Melody* (Richard Saunders, 1967), *You're Human like the Rest of Them* (B. S. Johnson, 1968), which was also bought by the BBC, *San Francisco* (Anthony Stern, 1969), which opened for an indefinite run at the Institute of Contemporary Arts weekend cinema in November 1970, and *One of the Missing* (Tony Scott, 1969). The latter, already in receipt of four awards, is a grim tragedy of the American Civil War, based on a short story by Ambrose Bierce. It was made with a Board grant of £800, while Scott was taking a post-graduate course in painting at Leeds College of Art. With the help of the grant he set up and shot the 26-minute film using fellow students and staff as cast (one of whom played five character parts, including a corpse), at Pately Bridge in the Yorkshire Dales. Films on painting and sculpture made in association with the Arts Council (*Magritte, Giacometti, Picasso – the Sculptor*) have continued to be a feature, and other subjects have ranged from the process of mortality (*You're Human Like the Rest of Them*, B. S. Johnson), ballooning, (*Man in the Clouds*, Patrick Beaver), to a number of Underground films. In *Outlook 1968* the Institute reported: "The most encouraging aspect of the Production Board's short history is the wealth of talent it has attracted. Designers, composers and technicians with experience in other media have been formed into teams to work on each production. The Board is overwhelmed by applicants, only a small minority of whom can be helped. It could use more money, but, in common with all producers of short films, its greatest headache is securing distribution, in order to allow more films to be made and to enable creative artists to realise their potential."

To date 1969 was the most productive year, with four international prizes secured, fourteen films completed, and two features in production.

"It is not always remembered," Bruce Beresford says, "that 90 per cent of all these films are *first* films – the first films their young makers have ever produced (and written, directed, edited, photographed and sound-tracked) in their lives. Critics, if they do not ignore them entirely, are often apt to tear them apart as if they were works by Buñuel or John Ford. Even *Sight and Sound* will cover a Festival at which our films have been shown without mentioning a single one. *San Francisco* was the *only* British entry to win a prize at Oberhausen in 1969 and was almost completely ignored; and when Nina Hibbin did give it a full-scale review for *The Times*, the newspaper promptly went on strike!"

6

Distribution

1. THE FILM DISTRIBUTION LIBRARY

The Distribution Library and the Central Booking Agency, though separate units, are classed together as two of the main activities of the Film Services Division, along with the Regional Film Theatres. They represent the trading side of the Institute's work. The former grew out of the National Film Archive when it was realised that there was no point in preserving a vast quantity of film if *none* of it could ever be seen. In 1938 it was decided to make a certain number – as funds permitted – available for screening, and 16mm and 35mm copies were made of those selected, and were put into distribution by what was then known as the National Film Library. Basically the choice was guided by the intention to provide material which could present a history of the art of the cinema from its earliest days. In 1948 the Radcliffe Report recommended that this should be expanded, commenting that the existing collection of some hundred titles was "quite inadequate." The Report continued: "It has been put to us that, since there are some 400 sources from which non-theatrical films may be obtained and such a variety of sources is baffling to users, the Institute should undertake the distribution not only of the films in its own lending section, but of all films of this type."

In those early days all the Library's material was obtained direct from the Archive, of which it was an integral part. Gradually, however, it grew on its own impetus, began to acquire films from other sources, until eventually it developed into so large an organisation that it became completely independent, and now buys prints from the Archive in exactly the same manner as from elsewhere.

The working of the Distribution Library is similar to that of commercial distributors in the same category, except that most of its material is available only for private or non-commercial showing. With this restriction, anybody can hire a film on payment of a fee, the two main differences being (a) that the Library originated from the need to put into circulation items primarily necessary for film study, which was not particularly remunerative, and (b) that the charges are deliberately maintained at as low a level as possible, to encourage film societies, schools and similar bodies. Whereas the commercial distributor exists to make money, the BFI Film Distribution Library does not, and is under no obligation to cover its cost. From this it might appear that, as it widened its range, it might come into direct conflict with the industry, but in practice this does not result. The conditions of hire expressly state: "Films hired from the British Film Institute Distribution Library must not be exhibited to the general public or be used for any commercial purpose. Bookings are confirmed on the strict understanding that the location, type of audience and purpose of the show are as stated. No advertising is permissible in any way, outside the actual location, by press announcement or other form of publicity."

The basic principle of the Library is that, as John Huntley, head of Film Services, puts it, "we step in when a film is in danger of being lost. The industry looks on us as the suppliers of films which they don't want – in which they consider there is no longer any commercial interest. If, as sometimes happens, a film which has fallen out of favour (perhaps for quite a long period) has a sudden revival of interest, we drop out, and a commercial distributor will take it back. The situation, of course, changes frequently. In the early days few silent films were considered to have any value at all, and owners of pictures such as *Birth of a Nation*, *Intolerance*, *Metropolis*, *The Cabinet of Doctor Caligari* and *Way Down East* said 'Do what you like with them'. Then the advent of television revived interest in early films, and the situation changed completely. Added to this was the growing popularity of the silents encouraged by the NFT, and likely to increase with the opening of the second theatre, which ran a Silent Film Festival concurrently with the London Film Festival in 1970."

The BFI might, in fact, be said to have cut a small section of its own throat, were it not that money is no object (or at least not a primary one) and that its main aim is that, by whatever means, as many people as possible should see films. In certain cases a special arrangement will be arrived at with a commercial distributor, as happened in the case of the Russian silent classics. Movies such as *Potemkin*, *Mother* and *Strike* had been made available by the Library for up to twenty-five years, when an increasing public interest caused Contemporary Films to take them up: on account of the Library having kept them going for so long, however, it was allowed to continue distribution of the silent versions to schools and colleges, etc.

The Library has always been aware of its true function, and that there is an ever-present danger of pressure towards commercialism. In *Outlook 1966* it was stated: "The primary goal of the Film Distribution Library has been to establish a unique and comprehensive collection of films which effectively represent the history of the cinema. In the past few years two obstacles have prevented the Institute from reaching this goal. In the first place policy has been subjected to financial pressures, which have tended to swing the emphasis of the collection towards short films which make money: and there has been a danger of the revenue-earning aspects dominating the policy of the Distribution Library . . . Whilst the Institute has no objection to seeing services pay their way and contributing to other aspects of its work, it is obviously highly undesirable that commercial considerations should become dominant in film selection. . . . The second consideration concerns the question of rights, which has become increasingly important with the growing market provided by television and the consequent sales of even the oldest films to TV interests. Part of the original Distribution Library was based on the principle that certain silent films had, in effect, lost all commercial value and could therefore be distributed for use in education and by cultural organisations without fear of infringement of rights. The situation has now changed drastically. The Institute is in the position of having to negotiate the distribution rights on films which were once freely presented to it, and for which the owners were happy to have any form of circulation in order to keep alive the film and its actors for modern audiences. It is not going too far to say that the British Film Institute, through the National Film Theatre and the Distribution Library, has kept before the public the names of quite a number of artists and directors who are now enjoying a major revival."

Once again, it comes down to the question of money. The present budget (1969–70) of just under £5,000 is described by Philip Strick,* Head of Film Distribution, as ludicrously small for the national library of films on film history, particularly as, unlike the Film Production Board, the Library is not permitted to retain for its buying fund any profits it may make from its rentals – all has to go back to the Institute. "On this amount it is impossible to have any policy regarding the acquisition of films," Philip Strick continues, "and I know only too well there are plenty of enormous gaps in our lists. As always, it is a question of priorities. No one has ever been particularly generous to the Film Library: it has always been the Cinderella." (Ugly Sisters would appear to predominate to an unusual extent at the Institute!) The fact that the Library can only buy what it can afford, and as cheaply as possible also precludes competition with commercial interests.

On his methods of selection, Strick comments, "I see *every* film that comes my way, and look it over with two points in mind: (a) Has it a place in our Library? and (b) How successful is the film in what it sets out to do? Then I will discuss it with the maker and either offer to purchase it for the BFI Library or, if I think its chances are good enough, recommend a large number of alternative distributors where the film might more appropriately be placed or where the film-maker could probably get a better price. Our budget and the priorities of the Library both prevent our spending a great deal on the Production Board's films, but that is probably to their advantage. A film like *Loving Memory*, for instance, should definitely not be taken into the Library unless it has been turned down by every commercial distributor in Wardour Street – though with some forty regional theatres now operating the chances of a modest return from public screenings are much improved."

Occasionally the mere fact of negotiating for a film will place it out of the Library's reach. The once universally demanded *Bicycle Thieves* of De Sica had been out of circulation for many

* *See page 182.*

Harold Lloyd at the opening of the Leeds RFT, 1970

Darling, Do You Love Me?, directed by Martin Sharp

STILL FROM THE FILM PRODUCTION BOARD

Herostratus, directed by Don Levy

STILL FROM THE FILM PRODUCTION BOARD

years, and it might have seemed that public interest had lapsed, but when the Library asked after it the producers began to think there must be a reviving market for it, and put it up for auction, with the result that it was taken over by Contemporary.

Totally distinct from the renting section is the sales side of the department. The BFI has some 500 films to sell, including its own production total of some 100 titles.* The selling process can be a lengthy business, as it can take several years to sell one film thoroughly throughout the world. There was a useful break-through, however, in the autumn of 1970, when Films Incorpo-rated bought over seventy titles, including the Arts Council productions distributed internationally through the BFI, and agreed also to take the Production Board's total output for the next seven years. The world-wide circulation of *The War Game* (see p. 48) through Philip Strick's office provided a considerable number of international distribution contacts from which the Institute's sales operations have continued to benefit.

Yet another aspect of the distribution department that has become emphasised in recent years is that in which it acts as a form of distributing mechanism for a number of organisations, notably Gala Films, Connoisseur Films (incorporating the films of the Academy Cinema), Amanda, and others. The BFI stores, services and despatches films in accordance with their instructions, for which a small fee is charged. Thousands of films pass through the hands of the Institute every year as a result of all these activities. Films are daily imported for the NFT, the Archive and the regions; at the same time they are daily sent out on all gauges to cinemas, universities, colleges, schools and societies.

Despite financial stringency, the Distribution Catalogue (as comprehensive and admirably produced a publication as the Archive Catalogues already mentioned) offers a wide range of both subjects and titles. "The core of the Distribution Library," says the Foreword, "is the unique collection of films illustrating cinema history." Apart from the classics, which one would

---

* The term 'film sales' in this context can cover long-term lease to television companies, sales of prints to other libraries, or outright purchase of a copy by a private collector. No copyright goes with such a transaction, which means that the private owner cannot resell his print, nor show it publicly, nor copy or rent it.

expect to find, are such silent features as Thomas Ince's *Civilisation* (1916), Griffith's *True Heart Susie* (1919), King's *Tol'able David* and Feyder's *L'Atlantide* (1921), L'Herbier's *The Late Mathias Pascal* and the rare Chaney *Phantom of the Opera*, Colleen Moore in *Ella Cinders* (1926), Kinugasa's *Crossways* (1928), Anthony Asquith's *Shooting Stars* (1928) and *A Cottage on Dartmoor* (1929), the German *People on Sunday* (Siodmak and Ulmer, 1929), Ozu's *I was Born, But . . .* (1932): and in sound, the early musical *Lucky Boy*, with George Jessel (directed by Norman Taurog, 1928), the British *Music Hall* (directed by John Baxter, 1934), Reinhardt's *Midsummer Night's Dream* (1935), Lang's *You Only Live Once* (1937), Hawks' *Bringing Up Baby* (1938), Ford's *Informer* and *Stagecoach* (1935 and 1939), Welles' two masterpieces, *Citizen Kane* and *The Magnificent Ambersons* (1941 and 1942), Lubitsch's *To Be or Not To Be* (1942), Sjoberg's *Frenzy* (1944), Crichton's *Painted Boats* (1945), Huston's *African Queen* (1951) and *Beat the Devil* (1953), Buñuel's *El* (1952), Bergman's *Sawdust and Tinsel* (1953) and *Journey Into Autumn* (1955), Wajda's *The Siberian Lady Macbeth* (1961). Of note are several early Hitchcocks, *The Lodger*, *The Ring*, *Murder*, *Blackmail*, etc. A valuable acquisition during 1969–70 was Buñuel's masterpiece *L'Age d'Or*, which had been out of circulation for a number of years; another, by special arrangement with Hungarofilm, was the first production of Istvan Szabo, *The Age of Daydreaming*.

Historical shorts and documentaries start with *The Kiss* (1896), include a considerable number of early Chaplins, Lloyd in his Lonesome Luke character, Mack Sennett and other comedies, the misleadingly titled "compilation films" (in reality compressed versions) of Barrymore's *Dr Jekyll and Mr Hyde*, *The Three Musketeers*, *Orphans of the Storm*, *Nosferatu* and others, up to Nazi films for students and the latest BFI productions. There are films on sculpture and painting (a particularly wide choice), architecture and experiments in visual art, and a series of true 'compilations' of historical cinematic interest – suggested history programmes, critical and technical shorts, study extracts and units. A number of films from the Canadian Film Board are available, including a study of Buster Keaton at work while making one of his last films, *The Railrodder*. There are also several subdivisions – Specialised

Film Libraries, movies made by children and amateurs, sections on transport, war history, education, and from the Nuffield Foundation, University College London Film Archive and other sources. Chief of these subsidiaries is the Science Library of around 500 titles, for which a separate catalogue is issued. Selected with the assistance of the British Universities Film Council, the titles in the Science Library are research films and documentaries ranging from historical records to reports on contemporary developments in all fields of medicine, physics, chemistry, mathematics and psychiatry. Recent additions include such titles as *Action of Involute Gear Teeth*, *Bird Migration*, *Congenital malformations of the Heart*, *Daphnia*, *Computer Aided Building Design*, *Were Ni – He is a Madman* (study of primitive treatment of psychiatric disorder among a Western Nigerian Tribe), *Cambridge Multiple-Access System*, *Regional Anaesthesia of the Hind Foot of the Ox*, *Two- and Three-Year-Olds in Nursery School* and *Why Does a Flea Jump?* The BFI also acts as United Kingdom distributing agent for a number of American organisations making research films, among them Scientific America, Appleton-Century-Crofts and the New York University Film Library.

To this list, the Gala Catalogue adds over forty major feature films, representing directors such as Bresson (*Au Hasard, Balthazar*), Godard (*Masculin-Feminin, Pierrot Le Fou*), Truffaut (*Jules et Jim, Les Quatre Cents Coups*), Resnais (*La Guerre est Fini*), Clouzot (*Les Diaboliques*), Fellini (8½), and a dozen or so from Ingmar Bergman, including *The Face*, *The Seventh Seal*, *The Silence*, *Smiles of a Summer Night*, *Winter Light* and *Wild Strawberries*.

Popularity prediction is difficult, except for the obvious classics, a run on Chaplin and Laurel and Hardy at Christmas, etc. A series of shorts from Granada aimed at the fifteen to sixteen age group entitled *The Facts are These* and dealing with sex education, smoking, drugs and similar matters is regularly asked for, as is another Granada production on *Management*. A surprise success has been the large collection of films on painting and sculpture, including those selected and made by the Arts Council. Pride of place for all time goes to Peter Watkins' *The War Game* referred to earlier. There is no doubt whatever that the Distribution Library performs a vital function, within its financial limits, in keeping alive valuable films (not only the 'greats') which, if they had to rely on commercial care, would surely die.

2. THE CENTRAL BOOKING AGENCY

Though often confused with the Film Distribution Library, the CBA has in fact no connection with it, except insofar as they are two separate units in the Film Services Division of the BFI. The CBA is simply what its name implies – an agency through which film societies can book the titles they require, whether from the BFI Library or from any other source in the United Kingdom. The purpose of the agency's existence is to save time and trouble and to proffer advice and help. Use of these services is restricted to members of the Agency, which is independent of BFI membership. There are in Britain dozens of organisations from whom it is possible to hire film, and many film societies and educational bodies have neither the time nor the opportunity to wade through the mass of catalogues available. For a charge of 10 per cent of the cost the CBA will book the film or films from the distributor or library concerned, arrange for its despatch, chase it up or arrange for a substitute if it is lost in transit, undertake an initial accountancy service, and provide programme notes together with details of its length and other technical matters. The convenience of this service is obvious, particularly when, as is usually the case, a society or college is presenting a programme of items which are owned by a number of different companies. All that is necessary in such a case is for the entire list to be sent to the CBA, who will do the rest. Members are, of course, free to deal direct with distributors should they wish to do so, and it is important to note that individual private hirers are not eligible for Agency membership.

In theory a purely mechanical organisation, the Agency is in fact often asked for advice as to the selection of films – particularly where there is a choice of several on one non-fictional subject. It could be said to work in a dual advisory capacity: (a) it can recommend a film to a society or other body, and (b) on the other side of the fence, it can, as a result of enquiries it has received, give a film distributor an estimate of the amount of bookings he might expect to receive for any particular item. It publishes a yearly catalogue, 'Films on Offer', which lists the productions of which it has the highest opinion and it holds viewing sessions from time to time at the NFT and elsewhere to enable potential bookers to form their own opinions on a number (necessarily small) of its selections.

To add a spice of complication, the CBA also owns a small number of films itself, numbering some seventy titles – both shorts and features – including de Sica's *The Children are Watching Us*, Autant-Lara's *Sylvie and the Ghost*, *Tribute to Richard Massingham*, and the Polish short *Hospital*, Hubley's *Harlem Wednesday* and other animation films.

The extensive use made of the CBA can be seen from the number of bookings a year – 16,966 during 1969–70, and there is no doubt that, despite its mechanistic framework, it must inevitably exercise a selective (and, it is hoped, salutary) influence on which films flourish in the large non-commercial market.

7

Publication

1. SIGHT AND SOUND

Sight and Sound began its existence one year before the BFI (Vol. 1, No. 1 appearing in Spring 1932) as "A Quarterly Review of Modern Aids to Learning", published under the auspices of the British Institute of Adult Education. The editorial of No. 3 hailed excitedly "A Film Institute within Sight"! – and by 1933–4 the BFI had both arrived and taken it over – and reduced the price from 1s to 6d. The periodical was presented with a new-look cover, but was not otherwise greatly changed. Even during its pre-Institute days, despite its educational basis,* it devoted an appreciable amount of space to feature and fiction films. The index to the first volume contained over a hundred entertainment film titles as against about forty educational. It is interesting to glance at C. A. Lejeune's list of "films you ought to see" in the first issue: *Westfront 1918; Kameradschaft; Congress Dances; Un Soir de Rafle* (what happened to that one?); *A Nous La Liberté; Tabu;* and *Round the World in 80 Minutes* (Douglas Fairbanks Snr.). In No. 3 she considered *Grand Hotel* "probably the best value for money the commercial talkie has ever produced."

Other reviewers in those days included Paul Rotha and Alistair Cooke, writing in a 'Films of the Quarter' series, and as time went on more and more attention was paid to the film as an end in itself as well as an educational tool. Items by film-makers appeared (including, in 1938, an interesting article by Meliés written just before his death), together with surveys on the cinema in countries throughout the world. Even so, the emphasis continued to be on films in education rather than education in the film – for example, the eight-page supplement starting in 1934, which has already

* A proposal was put forward that it should accept no advertisements of commercial films unless they had a "definite educational value".

been referred to. At this time, sales were restricted to members of
the Institute, and in 1938 the financial position showed a lost of
£450.

With the outbreak of war the magazine narrowly escaped
extinction. Proposals were made, first to suspend publication
altogether, then to amalgamate it with the *Monthly Film Bulletin*.
Fortunately it was finally permitted to retain its identity. As if
adapting itself to that black winter, it abruptly exchanged its
cover for one of more austere appearance, but retained its 6d
price. It made a brief return to a more cheerful look, but in 1941
succumbed to wartime pressure – shrinking to half its page size
and losing its illustrations for the duration. The policy remained
much the same, except for the limitations of subject natural in the
existing conditions. A new feature, 'News from the Societies',
started in 1941.

About a year after the war, in 1946, *Sight and Sound* returned
to its original size, and to a worthy, but to be honest somewhat
stodgy format. Stills were back, but infrequent and, though
respectably large, not very well reproduced. One notable point,
however, was the very full coverage in those days of books,
magazines and other publications, both English and foreign. The
turn of policy towards the art and entertainment film, accelerated
no doubt by the Radcliffe Report, continued. During 1948 the
'Film in Education' supplement disappeared as a separate section,
and about the same time the name of the editor – which had
hitherto remained coyly in hiding from the contents page –
appeared: R. W. Dickinson.

Towards the end of 1949, following the Report and as a result
of Denis Forman's determination to invigorate the magazine,
Sight and Sound took on a new look, and became more like the
publication as it is today. It also appeared monthly, retaining the
price of 2s 6d from after the war. For the first time, it went out on
public sales. The build-up took some years, but by 1958 circulation
figures had reached 15,000. The whole look and tone of the magazine became a good deal livelier. The new editor was Gavin
Lambert, with Penelope Houston as assistant, and Lindsay Anderson, Wolf Mankowitz and Kenneth Tynan among the contributors. Lambert, Anderson and Penelope Houston had all been

connected previously with the famous and much-lamented *Sequence*. "*Sight and Sound* was run by a group of very bright people," says Denis Forman of those days, "and really took off as a publication. For my money, Ken Tynan has never written better than he did for *Sight and Sound*."

An entertaining feature which continued for several years was entitled 'The Seventh Art', quoting some of the wilder flights of inspired – and uninspired – idiocy indulged in by those connected with the world of film, somewhat after the style of the *New Statesman*'s well-known 'This England'. They were mostly too long to quote here, but it was nice to learn, for instance, that, according to *Modern Screen* "there is probably less sexual activity among actors and actresses as a group (*sic*) than among many others"; that Burt Lancaster was convinced that "the life-story of a stamp collector, dull as it sounds, could be made into rich and thrilling screen fare if it were told in terms of its actionful incidents"; that a plan for a film of Hiawatha was turned down by Hollywood because he was so much a peacemaker that such a picture might aid the Communist peace propaganda; that "according to Fritz Lang the camera is the primary difference between films and any other form of dramatic expression"; that Elia Kazan was "not a Shakespeare man – a lot of his plays are badly constructed and I'm not taken in by the poetry"; that Herbert Wilcox (talking of pay-as-you-see television) was sure "you wouldn't find the British public putting coins in the slot for anything that was unsavoury"; that *The Robe* – "the greatest story of love and faith ever told – stuns with its glory as it embraces the audience without the use of spectacles". The latter presumably was a side-swipe by the newly developed Cinema-Scope at its novelty rival 3D. It was interesting, also, to hear of the projectionist who helpfully tried to increase his productivity by running films through at high speed. Unfortunately this glint of gaiety in the sometimes rather grim and humourless business of film criticism and discussion was later dropped.

Another interesting series of the period was a monthly 'Re-valuation' of a well-known film of early years (*Mother*, *The Italian Straw Hat*, *Shooting Stars*, *Siegfried*, etc.) from the standpoint of the then present day. The articles were contributed mainly by Roger

Manvell. It would be as interesting again to see how a re-revaluation of the same classics would read today, twenty years later.

To celebrate the Festival of Britain, *Sight and Sound* issued a special number, "Films in 1951", comprising interviews with British film-makers and a well illustrated survey of "10 Years of British Films" by Sir Michael Balcon. Thereafter the magazine reverted to a quarterly issue (the monthly experiment having unfortunately not paid off), with an increase in size and a price of 3s 6d. For a few numbers it indulged in the horrible habit of two-colour paging – inserting sections on a sickly yellow paper – catching the disease perhaps from the French *Cahiers du Cinéma* of the time. Happily this aberration did not last long.

In 1952, as a sequel to an international Brussels Referendum on the "10 Best Films", *Sight and Sound* asked eighty-five critics from ten countries a similar question. The replies (from sixty-three resulted in the following choice:

1 *Bicycle Thieves*
2 *City Lights* and *The Gold Rush*
4 *Battleship Potemkin*
5 *Louisiana Story* and *Intolerance*
7 *Greed, Le Jour se Lève* and *The Passion of Joan of Arc*
10 *Brief Encounter, Le Million* and *La Règle du Jeu.*

Citizen Kane, La Grande Illusion and *The Grapes of Wrath* headed the runners-up. About ten years later another questionnaire was held, and a hundred critics from various countries were asked for their selections. Seventy replies were received, and the amalgamated list makes an interesting comparison with the earlier one:

1 *Citizen Kane*
2 *L'Avventura*
3 *La Règle du Jour*
4 *Greed, Ugetsu Monogatari*
6 *Battleship Potemkin, Bicycle Thieves, Ivan the Terrible*
9 *La Terra Trema*
10 *L'Atalante*

Runners-up were *Hiroshima, mon Amour, Pather Panchali* and *Zéro de Counduite. Intolerance* had dropped to sixth place among the runners-up. *The Birth of a Nation* was conspicuous by its absence on both occasions.

In June 1952 the magazine showed a profit for the first time. Two years later a prize of £50 was offered for the best design for a new cover. A change duly appeared the following year, but after only two issues this was altered again, and then retained for the following decade.

In 1956 Gavin Lambert left to go to Hollywood, first as assistant to Nicholas Ray, and then as script-writer and novelist. Through his stay in office the number of readers had increased considerably. "During the six-and-a-half years in which he edited this magazine," said the editorial reporting his departure, "its reputation has kept pace with its circulation. . . . Gavin Lambert was an adventurous editor as well as a discriminating one, a disciplined writer who retained the tough-minded individuality that is part of the legacy left by *Sequence*. *Sight and Sound* has reflected his enthusiasms – for the cinema and for good writing – and it is by these enthusiasms that its standards have been determined." Penelope Houston took over the editorship, a post she still holds, with David Robinson, later Peter John Dyer, and (from 1962 to 70) Tom Milne, as assistant.

The twenty-fifth anniversary of the BFI was celebrated by a special issue of *Sight and Sound* – all aglitter in silver cover – which included a full, illustrated index of the work of British directors. Throughout this period it had not changed its format or style to any great extent, but had steadily built up a reputation as one of the most influential and best produced minority periodicals on its subject in the world. This reputation, however was by no means unassailed. In 1956 the critical policy was attacked by the film industry, who suggested that it did not always appreciate the difficulties of film-making, and that its whole approach was too esoteric. It had always printed a disclaimer from the Institute of any responsibility for contributors' views, and a proposal was now made at a Governors' Meeting that the whole publication should become self-supporting and detached from the BFI altogether. The suggestion was not accepted, but it was to be raised again at a later date. Complaints were also made that it did not pay sufficient attention to British films. To this it replied, in its editorial of Autumn 1956. "If some readers believe, as an occasional letter in our correspondence columns suggests, that the magazine places over-much emphasis on foreign affairs, this is because its editorial policy has always and essentially been one of discovery."

The same complaints were raised again in 1961. Fears were expressed that the opinions of the contributors tended to be identified, especially overseas, with those of the Institute – and even the British Government – and it was suggested that the disclaimer should be more conspicuously displayed. Penelope Houston replied that the magazine was necessarily directed to a minority readership, but that it followed the policy of the Institute as a whole, i.e., to stimulate serious interest in the cinema.

In 1965 it was awarded the Plaquette Leone di S. Marco at the Venice Film Book Exhibition run in conjunction with the Festival. The cover had by this time taken on the appearance it was to keep until late 1970, a pleasant, unfussy lay-out which permitted the selected still to be well displayed. The price remained at 3s 6d until spring 1962, when it rose to 4s, to 4s 6d in spring 1965, and 5s in summer 1968. For winter 1970/1 a new and slightly larger format was designed, at a new and slightly larger price of 6s. Throughout the sixties the table of contents remained more or less unchanged, with sections of features, articles, film reviews and book reviews – the last two severely selective for a quarterly periodical. Sales reached 30,000 for the first time in 1969, 31,500 in 1970.

As it enters the seventies, *Sight and Sound* is again coming under fire, mainly for its alleged neglect of British film-makers and over-severe attitude towards their products, its generally lofty critical approach and its cosy coterie corners. To some extent all these complaints may be held to have some justification, though if one includes all the Round Table Conferences, Special Issue Indexes, etc., the actual space devoted to British cinema through the years would probably work out in fair proportion to the foreign output. On the other hand the lengthy accounts, especially around Festival times, of foreign titles, many of which the reader is unlikely to have any chance of seeing, can tantalise without satisfying, even if they are justified by the magazine's sub-title "The International Film Quarterly."

Reaction to criticism is an intensely personal matter and one's opinion of a critic is likely to be based largely on whether one agrees with his likes and dislikes. At least it can be said that *Sight and Sound* reviews are generally lengthy and leisured enough for the writer to have space in which to justify – or at least defend – his assertions of opinion. The higher reaches of film criticism seem particularly conducive to the production of hot air, and *Sight and Sound* probably contributes no more than a reasonable proportion of pseudo-profundities.* The question of highbrowism ultimately rests on the altitude of the reader's own brows. Where brow meets brow, all is peace and understanding. Taking the good with the bad, to read through *Sight and Sound's* thirty-nine volumes to date is to appreciate its unique importance as a record and commentary on the *whole* period of the film.

2. THE MONTHLY FILM BULLETIN

The first number of the MFB appeared in February 1934. Of its sixteen pages, fourteen were concerned with documentary or educational films, only two with 'entertainment' productions: of these, only the plot synopsis, certificate and distributor were given. A few months later an Entertainment Panel was set up to supervise the compilation of this section, and by the tenth number it had grown to eleven pages, and the details given of each film included director, stars, age-suitability and brief initialled reviews. From the start it has observed its function as primarily a work of reference, as complete a list as possible of every film as it became available in Great Britain. The educational films were provided with such information as Description, Teaching notes, Distributors, Conditions of Supply, Contents, Appraisal and Suitability. This general layout continued, with minor variations such as fuller technical credits for 'entertainment' films, until September 1949, though a "Notes of the Month" section was added in 1947 with brief reports of the activities of the BFI.

Like *Sight and Sound*, the *Monthly Film Bulletin* was showing a deficit in 1938, but unlike the former, there was never any

---

* "I happened to look at a copy of *Sight and Sound*," remarked Stanley Donen, the film director, "and you know, it's awfully highbrow!"

question of ceasing publication during the war. It was, however, forced to close its subscription list temporarily in 1945 owing to lack of paper supplies. In its early years the *Bulletin* was free from full members (associates paid 2d) and available only to them. By 1947 it was on sale at 1s 6d. In that year its ratio of contents was eight pages devoted to entertainment features, one to entertainment shorts, three to educational films and one to documentary and interest shorts. A radical change took place in September 1949, when the editorial stated: "With this issue, readers will notice changes in the presentation of the *Monthly Film Bulletin*, applying to both the Entertainment and the Educational and Informational film sections. In the first case, it is felt that to subject all feature films to the same form of review and analysis, to give every film a detailed synopsis and appraisal of content and technique, irrespective of its pretensions and purpose, is not the most logical way of criticism. It has been decided, therefore, that only films which make serious demands on the intelligence of audiences, which have a purpose beyond simple entertainment, shall be reviewed at length. Straightforward, unambitious entertainment films which make no real claims on critical faculties will be briefly noticed and classified purely from an entertainment point of view. In this way, it is hoped that it will be easier to distinguish between the two kinds of films, and that the criticisms will be fairer to both." This of course entailed selection: hitherto all entertainment films had received the same amount of attention. Longer notices were initialled as before, the shorter ones were criticised anonymously and graded I (good of its type), II (average) and III (poor). At the end of all reviews was an audience-suitability rating. Credits of all films received still fuller coverage, including full cast lists together with the names of characters played – an essential one would have expected to have found earlier. At the same time the reviewing of 'classroom films' was dropped, in accordance with the spirit of the Radcliffe Report, and this service was carried out by the newly formed *Visual Education*, published by the National Committee for Visual Aids in Education.

In January 1951 (Vol. 18, No. 204) the *Bulletin* appeared in its first red cover, and in layout was more or less as twenty years later – which in a reference-type publication is as it should be. Later in the year it went temporarily, and inexplicably, into three-column paging. The Newsletter ceased in 1952. The price rose to 2s.

April 1962 saw a change in cover design and also the start of a new feature, when a panel of critics (John Coleman, Paul Dehn, Peter John Dyer, John Gillett, Penelope Houston, Dilys Powell, David Robinson, Richard Roud and John Russell Taylor) allotted star ratings to a selection of the month's films. This ran into trouble with the trade, who asked that a statement be made that such assessments did not necessarily reflect popular response – a reassurance one would have thought hardly necessary. Eventually the panel was discontinued, though it was later revived.

An extremely useful occasional feature was started in 1963, consisting of a Checklist on the complete record of a particular film-maker's work – director, actor, cameraman, script-writer, editor. The series started with Lindsay Anderson in April, and has since covered, among others, Louise Brooks, Orson Welles, Dirk Bogarde, Carol Reed, Jean-Luc Godard, John Huston, Douglas Slocombe, Martin Ritt, George Cukor, Anouk Aimée, James Wong Howe, Michel Simon, Jerzy Lipman, Katherine Hepburn, Claude Chabrol, Lee Garmes, and a two-part dictionary of Italian pseudonyms, reaching a total, by the end of 1970, of sixty-three lists.

In September 1968 the price was raised to 2s 6d, the 'suitability' rating dropped, and the Critics' Panel restarted. More importantly, the names of the main reviewers were given. Hitherto the reviews had been initialled, but with no key for reference this was a useless appendage. Unfortunately the shorter notices are still, at the time of writing, shrouded in anonymity.*

At the same time the name of the film director was given more prominence by being set at the head of the credits. This also proved helpful – once one had learnt not to go hunting for it in the old place. Apart from the year 1969, when an unfortunate choice of dark blue for the cover endangered the eyesight of anyone trying to read the table of contents, the format remained unchanged until the increase to larger size at the end of 1970. In the 1969–70

* From January 1971 all reviews are named.

financial year the *Bulletin* reviewed a record number of 420 films – sales remaining steady at 10,000 copies per issue.

As with *Sight and Sound*, criticism has been levelled against the *Bulletin* at various times owing to the tone of some of the reviews, which were described in 1961 as "mannered and unfair", and it does seem that the hitherto faceless writers of the short notices in particular are not easy to please. The ordinary filmgoer returning innocently happy from some less-than-masterpiece may well find himself glancing furtively into his *Bulletin* to see whether he should have had such a pleasant evening, and end up guiltily conscious of being severely admonished for having enjoyed himself. On the other hand it is easy to understand that the reviewer, faced with a gelatinous mass of monthly mediocrity, may well at times regard the cinema screen with a jaundiced eye.

It is as a work of reference, however, that the *Bulletin* (edited at present by Jan Dawson, who took over from David Wilson at the end of 1970) must be finally judged, and in this respect it is unique and indispensable, particularly from the time when it enlarged its listing of credits. Its unbroken run from its inception (during the printing dispute of 1950 it was brought out by a photographic process) makes it an invaluable asset for anyone working on or interested in the history of the cinema. One can only regret that it had not been started twenty years previously.

3. OTHER PUBLICATIONS

The BFI has always been prolific in the production of books, pamphlets and papers. The ill-fated *Contrast* and the early broadsheets have already been referred to, and another cause for regret was the cessation of a series of Indexes devoted to a particular director, formerly issued as supplements to *Sight and Sound*. A new and more elaborate series, illustrated by stills, was started in 1950 with Ebbe Neergaard on *Carl Dreyer*, and this was followed by studies of *Marcel Carné*, *Frank Capra*, *Jean Vigo* and *Anthony Asquith*, with two later additions (still available) on *René Clair* and *Max Ophuls* (1958). Difficulties of distribution were encountered – they were not, for instance, the type of publication which could be sold through the commercial bookshops – and the series ceased.

To some extent they have been superseded by *Cinema One* books (q.v.) and similar works from other sources such as Studio Vista, and Peter Cowie's series of books which developed from his International Film Guides, but as small-scale inexpensive reference books the Indexes were useful, and their demise was a pity.

Fifty Famous Films (1915–1945), from the NFT and based on their programme notes, was also a handy booklet. Another, on the "next most famous fifty" in the period before the *Monthly Film Bulletin* would be welcome, as would additions to their Folio Series – collections of about thirty stills, ten inches by eight in size, very well reproduced, and at 5s an inexpensive way of acquiring these often rare and costly items. So far only two have appeared, on *Buster Keaton*, and *Fifty Years of Soviet Cinema*. From the Archive came a useful technical work on *Film Preservation* (1965) originally prepared by the Preservation Committee of the IFFA. There are also the various catalogues previously described, and the NFT programme brochures have long been models of their kind, and worthy of preservation.

The majority of the Institute's publications come under the auspices of the Education Department, and include titles on *Film Teaching* and *Film and General Studies*, on directors such as *Fellini* (by Suzanne Budgen), *Don Siegel* (Alan Lovell) and *Budd Boetticher* (Jim Kitses), apart from a number of seminar papers in duplicated form, some of which are available for teachers and students free of charge.

Finally, a most important project was the launching of the *Cinema One* series. For this, as the Publications Department had no separate capital, Penelope Houston arranged a deal with the publishers Secker and Warburg, and later with Thames and Hudson, in which the financial risks to the BFI would be minimal. The Education Department, who receive a separate publication budget, were also anxious to issue a series of books. In order to avoid unnecessary duplication, however, a decision was arrived at to join forces, each individual volume to be edited by the department concerned, the joint publishers being the BFI and (at present) Thames and Hudson. The books are 'made-to-last' paperbacks, fully illustrated, on individual film-makers or other aspects of the cinema. Fourteen titles have so far appeared, among

Loving Memory, with Rosamund Greenwood and David Pugh, directed by Tony Scott

Still from the Film Production Board

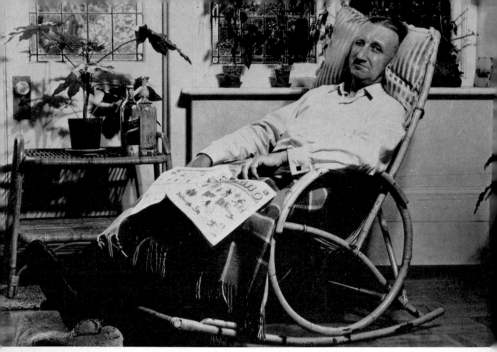

Stanley Reed, Director of the BFI, convalescing (with suitable
literature and medicine) from a coronary in 1966

Members of the staff "carry on" during his absence

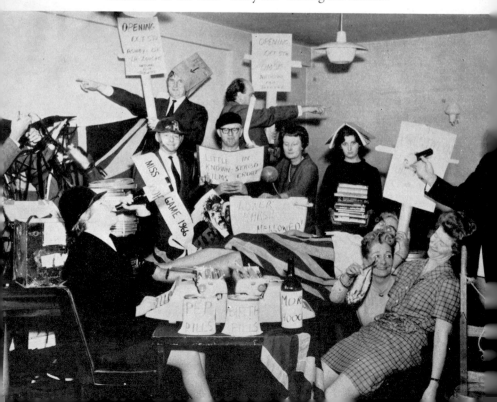

them *Buster Keaton* (David Robinson), *Rouben Mamoulian* (Tom Milne), *Hollywood Cameramen* (Charles Higham) and *How It Happened Here* (Kevin Brownlow) from *Sight and Sound*: and, from the Education Department *Howard Hawks* (Robin Wood), *Pasolini on Pasolini* (edited by Oswald Stack) and *The New Wave* (edited by Peter Graham).

Reports, summaries, outlooks, analyses, plans, declarations of intentions, statements of hopes, expressions of fears, even confessions of failures, have always poured forth in profusion. The BFI may sometimes have been shortsighted, or even hard of hearing – it could never be accused of being dumb.

M

8

Film Societies

As we have already seen, the link between the early British Film Institute and the film societies was a close one. It could be said that the Institute itself, though formed as a new organisation, had its genesis in the London Film Society. As it grew, provincial societies already existing (of which there were not very many) became affiliated to it, and as noted added the word 'Institute' to their titles – new ones were formed on the same principles. The film society itself was developing out of its old-time pattern of a visit to a cinema on Sundays when films were shown which were not otherwise available.

In the autumn of 1934 the Scottish Film Council was formed as an integral part of the BFI but with a larger degree of autonomy than was usual with Institute branches. In 1941 the attenuated *Sight and Sound* started a regular feature under the title "News from the Societies." Writing in 1955, Denis Forman recorded the remarkable growth of the film society movement since the war. "In 1939 there were eighteen societies, many of them veterans of seven or eight years' standing. During the war new societies sprang up to serve the special needs of wartime concentrations; many of these died as the population ebbed back into the peace-time pattern. In 1946, however, there were forty-eight societies, and since that date a sharp but steady rise has brought the number up to the remarkable figure of 230, serving an audience of perhaps 50,000 people."*

In March 1945, representatives of the film societies in England and Wales met in London for the purpose of forming a central organisation to protect and further their interests. This organisation, now known as the British Federation of Film Societies and

* *The Film and the Public* (Supplement).

incorporating Scotland, had its first meeting in September of that year, when a constitution was adopted. The Chairman was Major E. J. Eames, and the Secretary Oliver Bell. Six societies were elected to membership of the Executive Committee: Bradford Civic Playhouse, Leicester, Merseyside, Norwich, Oxford University and Swansea. Denis Forman:* "The success of the film society movement has been largely built upon the work of a small band of enthusiasts. Such people as Forsyth Hardy and Margaret Hancock (to mention but two), themselves running flourishing societies, found time to plan and carry through the development into federation with its attendant opportunities for nation-wide participation. . . . Much of the credit for the successful realisation of the film society schemes lies with these two bodies [i.e. the Scottish and the English and Welsh Federations]; standing in the background however, the Film Institute has provided moral support and from time to time financial help."

Since that time the movement has continued its rapid growth. In 1958 the total number of societies was approximately 400, today there are some 750 – all of them run on a voluntary basis. Throughout the years the relationship between the Institute and the societies has been one of slightly guarded respect. While ready to acknowledge its debt to the Institute, and appreciative of the facilities it offered, the Federation has always kept careful watch over its independence. The alliance has been at times an uneasy one.

The National Film Theatre had, as we have seen, little to offer (or threaten, depending on the viewpoint) the provinces. When the idea of regional theatres began to cast a shadow, however, the attitude of some societies was distinctly cautious. There was apprehension that they might lose their identity, or be swallowed up should such a theatre be started in their district.

In 1966 a conference was held at Andover by the Federation, at which fundamental issues of policy were discussed. During the past year the Federation, representing some 400 members, had made it clear that it considered its own thinking had remained static too long. *Outlook 1966* reported: "The Autumn, 1965, issue of *Film*, the magazine published by the Federation of Film Societies, carried a leading article which commented that: 'The

* *The Film and the Public* (Supplement).

film theatres in the provinces and the regional centres could provide the backbone of a completely rejuvenated [film society] movement'. Film societies, it went on, 'should be contributing to this resurgence of film activity. They should be part of it; the mistake is to see themselves apart.' Earlier in the year, the Federation had approached the Institute with a view to defining a closer working relationship between the two organisations. Mr Stanley Reed, director of the Institute, attended the Federation's Andover conference and took a line similar to that of the *Film* editorial, in urging higher standards of presentation and a more aggressive policy in seeking those local subsidies on which film societies (like any other form of cultural organisation) may have a claim."

The BFI appointed a Film Society Liaison Officer, who also serves as Secretary of the Federation, and provided the Federation with permanent office accommodation and use of all facilities. Member societies can obtain films from the Distribution Library at 25 per cent discount: the Central Booking Agency provides a booking service for films from any source in Britain; and also offers advice and help on programming and on commercial and technical problems, besides publishing the catalogue "Films on Offer". Member societies also have the use of the Lecture Service. The Federation (which since 1969 has represented all *bona-fide* societies) issues its own news letter and other sources of information to its members, and runs its own viewing sessions.

Doubtless the British Federation of Film Societies will continue to keep a wary eye on any developments which it considers may become an infringement of its autonomy. "We're completely independent of the BFI, you know, even if our offices are in the same building," is the reply likely to meet any query which seems to imply a link between the two organisations. However, the deliberate attempt made mutually at Andover to come closer together, and the ease of communication resulting from work in the same building, undoubtedly paved the way to a smoother relationship. In practice, the worst fears concerning the effects of regional development seem not to have been realised, and in many towns where theatres now operate they run harmoniously parallel with the film societies. After all, though the roads may be separate, they lead in the same direction.

9

The Future

One has to draw a line somewhere, and we have now followed the story of the BFI up to the early months of 1971. Many plans are already going ahead, however, for the coming year, and most of them will probably have come to realisation by the time this book appears in print.

Five new Regional Theatres are expected to be running by November, at Swindon, Grays (Essex), Stirling, Harlow and Lancaster.

The money has been voted for the National Film School, which will ensure the start of what has every appearance of being an undertaking of prime importance.

For the first time, the Film Production Board is to have a share of Eady Money (the British Film Fund Agency) – a token allocation of £10,000 for the year. Added to other allocations, this will bring the total funds available to £30,000, a considerable increase over the current £12,500.

The NFT Restaurant building is now complete, extending from the old foyer under Waterloo Bridge towards the river. The smallest of the theatres, NFT 3, is already in use for receptions and other gatherings; showing from its verandah a view of the Thames to rival that from the Royal Festival Hall further along the bank.

In the John Player Lecture Series Richard Attenborough gave a highly successful retrospective account of his all-round career in the cinema, guided by Dilys Powell. Claude Chabrol also appeared, and on 28th February John Trevelyan, retiring censor, made his final appearance in his official capacity – but not, it is to be hoped, as a layman. David Niven, Shirley MacLaine, Rex Harrison, Jean Rouch, Richard Fleischer and Terence Rattigan were scheduled for the spring and early summer. The proposed extension of the Lectures to the Region was started during the summer months, with Charlton Heston first on the list.

An interesting widening in the scope of the John Player programmes is a series of talks and discussions held in the smaller NFT 2 under the general title "Aspects of Cinema": dealing, as Brian Baxter, in charge of programme planning for the cinema, puts it, with the technical, non-glamorous side of the cinema. Titles include Colin Young (Director of the National Film School) on "The New Film and the New Reality"; John Huntley on "Music in the Film", Roy Knight on "Film Teaching" and Lutz Becker on "Nazi Architecture in Film".

Tony Scott's *Loving Memory* was screened at the 1971 Cannes Festival, and afterwards shown in Paris.

In the same year Bruce Beresford retired from the Film Production Board to produce a film in his native Australia, and Philip Strick left the Distribution Department to join a firm of cassette consultants.

The *Monthly Film Bulletin* and *Sight and Sound* have both appeared in their new format, the *Bulletin* for the first time sporting a still on its cover, and abandoning the somewhat invidious "shorter reviews" division for a simple alphabetical listing of films throughout.

Finally, as this chapter goes to press Sir William Coldstream has made known his intention of resigning from the post of Chairman of the Board of Governors which he has held during the busy and progressive period 1964–71. His successor has not yet been named.* What changes of policy, if any, this will entail is also shrouded in the mists – or fogs – of the future. One thing, however, is certain: given the cash and resources which it needs in an increasingly costly *milieu* the British Film Institute will continue, in the future as in the past, making mistakes and learning from them, incurring criticism and receiving praise, falling short of some objectives and achieving others, dropping bricks and building on hopes – behaving, in fact, like any organisation in a healthy state of life and activity. To repeat (because they are the real crux of the matter) Stanley Reed's words from the first part of this book: "Everything we hope to accomplish is restricted by lack of funds – everything we have accomplished has been in spite of this."

⋆ THE NEW CHAIRMAN

In April 1971 it was announced that the new Chairman of the Institute would be Denis Forman, Joint Managing Director of the Granada Group and of Granada Television – to take office on 1st May. Denis Forman is the first Chairman of the Board of Governors to have held a former post (Director, 1949–55) in the BFI. The advantages of this prior connection are obvious. "I may not know a very great deal about present problems yet," he says, "but at least I know what they were in my time, and am familiar with the basic set-up." Before becoming Director Denis Forman had been in the Central Office of Information as a film-maker, taking charge of a production team under Miss Helen de Moulpied, whom he afterwards married, and later becoming Chief Production Officer. Mrs Forman herself has been a Governor of the BFI since 1965. It is as yet early days for new plans to be formulated, but it is very possible that by the time this book is published the outline of Things to Come will be taking Shape. "The film and television scene in the seventies is completely different from the one I knew in the fifties," says Forman. "It's more sophisticated, less monolithic, and the small screen is doing a lot of what used to be done on the big one. But it seems to me that the Institute's job is just as important as ever it was, perhaps more so."

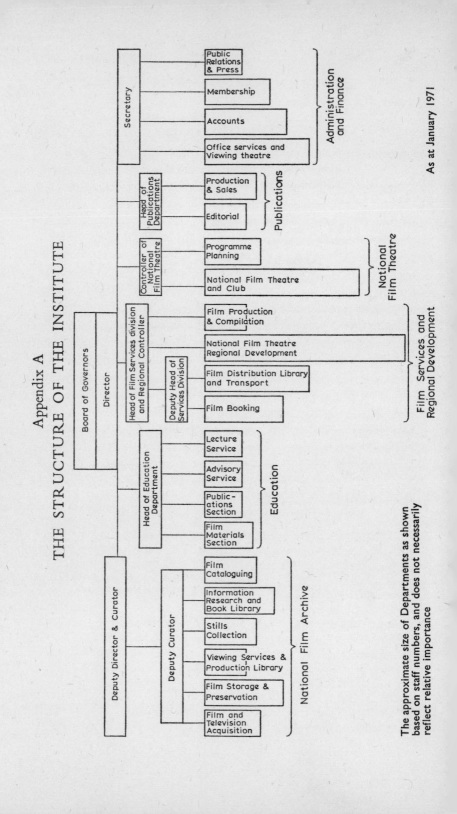

Appendix A

THE STRUCTURE OF THE INSTITUTE

As at January 1971

The approximate size of Departments as shown based on staff numbers, and does not necessarily reflect relative importance

APPENDIX B

CHAIRMEN OF THE BOARD OF GOVERNORS OF THE BFI

His Grace the Duke of Sutherland	1933–36
Sir Charles Cleland	1936–37
Sir George Clark	1938–39
Sir William Brass (later Lord Chattisham)	1939–45
Patrick Gordon Walker	1946–48
Cecil H. King	1948–52
S. C. Roberts	1952–56
Sylvester Gates	1956–64
Sir William Coldstream	1964–71
Dennis Forman	1971–

DIRECTORS OF THE BFI

J. W. Brown (as General Manager)	1933–36
Oliver Bell	1936–49
Denis Forman	1949–55
James Quinn	1955–64
Stanley Reed	1964–

GOVERNORS OF THE BFI (listed chronologically)

R. S. Lambert
Lady Levita
F. W. Baker
C. M. Woolf
Thomas Ormiston
A. C. Cameron
Colonel John Buchan
J. J. Lawson
L. J. Hibbert
J. Fairgrieve
Dr Benjamin Gregory
W. R. Fuller
Dr Percival Sharp
Hon. Eleanor Plumer

Professor W. Lyon Blease
M. Neville Kearney
Dr J. E. Smart
Sir Charles M. Barclay-Harvey
Sir Frederick Mander
Lieut. Colonel Sir Thomas Moore
Mrs Cazelet Keir
Sir W. Ross Barker
Captain Paul Kimberley
W. Glenvil Hall
Lady Apsley
Dr W. Alexander
E. G. Barnard
Sir Henry French

Professor B. Ifor Evans
Dr Winifred Cullis
Aidan Crawley
Frank Hill
J. H. Hoy
Lady Allen of Hurtwood
Sir Arthur Elton
Dilys Powell
Dr Stephen Taylor
Lady Tweedsmuir
Anthony Asquith
Mrs Eirene White
Norman Collins
J. M. Peddie
Mrs Holden
Mrs Jacquetta Priestley
I. J. Pitman
F. A. Ring
Frank A. Hoare
Sir George R. Barnes
C. A. Oakley
Norman Wilson
D. E. Griffiths
W. A. J. Lawrence
Basil Wright
Dr. John Brown
Angus Maude
Sir Michael Redgrave
Mrs Walter Elliot
Woodrow Wyatt
Hamish Hamilton
Sir Robert Bruce Lockhart
Ellis F. Pinkney
Robert Clark
Sir Wilfrid Eady
Arthur Abeles
Roy Jenkins
Mrs Isabel Cormack
John Newsom
Alastair Dunnett
Gerald Beadle
Celia Johnson

John Rodgers
Neil Paterson
Charles Goldsmith
Sir Hamilton Kerr
David Johnston
John Davis
Sir David Evans
J. Fairfax-Jones
Lady Barnett
John Mills
F. Donachy
J. B. Frizell
R. J. Stopford
David Kingsley
A. Havelock Allen
Mrs A. Ward-Jackson
Llewelyn Ward
G. C. Seligman
Paul Adorian
Sir Michael Balcon
Karl Miller
Kenneth Adam
Edgar Anstey
Jill Craigie
Muir Matheson
Carl Foreman
Arthur Blenkinsop
Professor Roy Shaw
Mrs Helen Forman
Jocelyn Baines
Dr L. Kerr
George Reith
G. Singleton
George M. Hoellering
Montague Morton
Lord Lloyd of Hampstead
Kevin Brownlow
Robert S. Camplin
Karel Reisz
Lindsay Anderson
James S. Christie
Professor Asa Briggs

APPENDIX C

SEASONS AT THE NATIONAL FILM THEATRE

1953. Origins of the Western; Great Comedians -- The Silent Screen; German Cinema Classics; Mexican Programme; Hitchcock; Silent Film in Russia; De Sica; Silent Film in France; The Coronation; Ealing Comedy; Silent Film in Britain; He, She and It; Documentary Tradition; Beginnings of the Cinema; Chaplin Programme; Christmas Comedy.

1954. Erich von Stroheim – Director and Actor; Carol Reed and Humphrey Jennings; Ballet; Gaumont-British Library Anniversary; The Child Actor; British and American Musical; World Cinema; Films from Asia; 50 Years of Film; Musicals.

1955. From the Stage to the Screen; Musicals and Comedies; W. C. Fields; Laurel and Hardy; Homage to United Artists; Luis Buñvel; Special; Cukor and Lang; Méliès and 4 Comedies; John Huston; Sixty Years of Cinema; John Ford; Hitchcock Thrillers; Drama in the Big City; Fable, Fairytale and Fantasy.

1956. World Cinema; Without Frontiers; Jean Rouch; Free Cinema One; Tribute to Warner Brothers; World Cinema – Russia Panorama; Horror; True Face of India; Free Cinema Two; Olympic Films; Return to Life – Italian Realist Films; British View – 21st Anniversary for Rank Distributors.

1957. Samuel Goldwyn – Producer; Bogart; De Maupassant's Stories; Germany – Then and Now, I Max Ophuls, II Modern West German Scene, III German Directors in Hollywood, IV East German Scene; Living in the Present – Problems; Canada; Yugoslavian Scene; Light in the Japanese Window; Captive Cinema – Associate Rediffusion Documentaries; Contribution to Comedy – History; Literature on the Screen – History; An Amazing Year (1957); Golden Age of Screen Comedy.

1958. Report From Central Europe – Czechoslovakia/Poland/Hungary/East Germany; Aspects of Film History – I Editing; II History and Legend; III The Human Condition; British Comedy of the '30s; Amateur Cine World – Ten Best of 1957; Tribute to the Russian Theatre; Max Ophuls; Aspect of Film History – Country Life – City Life; Films with a Purpose; BFI Experimental Film Production Fund Films; Period and Costume Films; Use of Sound and Music; Films From Brussels; Jean Cocteau; Free Cinema Four and Five;

Tribute to Eisenstein and Griffith; Aspects of Film History; Lion's Roar – Tribute to MGM.

1959. Tribute to William Wyler; DEFA Story (East German Film Monopoly); 21st Anniversary of the Boulting Brothers; Cinema Today – Italy; Polish Film School (Lodz); Last Free Cinema; Passionate Cinema – Films from Sweden; Visual Persuaders; 8-Day Forum on Cinema and tv as art and communication; Negro World; 30 Years of British Documentary; Robert Donat – An English Actor; Eisenstein and Pudovkin; Experiment in Britain; 100 Clowns; Four Musicals.

1960. Prague – London – A Czech Viewpoint; Films From the Archives; Entertainment Films of the '20s; Archive Connoisseur Series; French Season; Holiday Children's Programme; Orson Welles; Beat Square and Cool (USA); Joseph Mankiewicz; The Face of Asia – China Discovery; A Season of Ballet; Silver Jubilee; Poland; The New Generation; Pioneer of the New Wave – Jean-Pierre Melville; Comedy at Christmas; Roger Vadim.

1961. Antonioni; The Western; Archive Films; Entertainment Films of the '20s; British Film Academy Awards; Pabst and Murnau; American Thrillers; British Thrillers of the '30s; Jumpin' at the NFT; Square Pegs; Coming of the Talkies; Years Between (American Cinema 1940–1953); Visconti; New Talent from the Argentine; The Second Sex (Films on Women); Gary Cooper – 1901–1961; Entertainment Films of the '20s; The Stars; Leopoldo Torre-Nilsson; Joseph Losey; Nicholas Ray; Midwinter Blood; Early Chaplin.

1962–63. Fritz Lang; Top Ten; Midwinter Blood (Horror); Renoir; Fritz Lang; Minnelli I and II; Jean Renoir II; Art of Persuasion; Anarchist Cinema; Film Theatre Firsts (NFT discoveries over 10 years); The First World War; Dovzhenko and the Thirties; One Shots; Festival of Wild Life Films; Howard Hawks; Laurel and Hardy; Experimental Film Fund Films; David Lean – Sam Spiegel; Left Bank; British Film Academy Awards Short List; School of Vienna; Humphrey Bogart; Prepared Mirror; Top Eight; Ten Best; Satire; Frederico Fellini; King Vidor; The Real Avant-Garde; Yasujiro Ozu; Kenji Misoguchi; Eisenstein.

1963–64. But Not Forgotten; Report from Poland; George Stevens; Rex Harrison; Critic's Choice; Exchange Programmes of Russian Cultural and Scientific Films; British Film Academy Awards; The Thirties; Germany; Tribute to Robert Hamer; Rich and Strange; Top Eight; Ten Best; Music and Film; The Other Tradition; Heritage of Expressionism; The Thirties; Britain; Treasures of the Royal Belgian Film Archive; 50 Years of Hal Roach, Producer; 40 Years of Edward G. Robinson, Actor; 30 Years of Fred Zinnemann, Director; Charles Chaplin; Tih Minh to James Bond – A season of Spy Films.

1964–65. Tih Minh to James Bond – A season of Spy Films (2nd part); Encore – Will Hay and Laurel and Hardy; Out of Circulation;

Home Again; New Swedish Season; Preston Sturges; Czech Week; Marx Brothers; Mae West; Greek Cinema; Franju; Gance; Best From Danish Film Museum – Part One; Dreyer – Part One; Buñuel – Part One; Jazz Programme I and III; London Schools Film-making; 25 Years of British Animation; Films from Holland; Commonwealth Film Festival; Laurel and Hardy; Italian Cinema Archive; Best from the Danish Film Museum; Two Goldwyn Classics; Dreyer and Christensen; Jazz at the NFT; Buñuel; Films from Holland; An Old-Time British Cinema Programme 1914; Ninth London Film Festival; Buster and Beckett; Tribute to Josef von Sternberg; Satyajit Ray; Best of Busby Berkeley; Eight Days of Otto; Sophia Loren.

1966. Film of Joseph Losey; Renoir (Part Three); Play Into Film; The War Game; Masks and Faces – Great Stage Actors; Another Night in an English Musical Hall; Paris 56/66; Monday Night – Screen Acting; The Several Sides of Kon Ichikawa; The Paramount Style; Screen Acting; Underworld America; H. G. Wells; Screen Acting; Amateur Top Eight; London Film Festival 10; Many Strange Fancies; Film City (Sofia); Tribute to Mary Field OBE; Best of Elstree; Screen Acting.

1967. Why 1066; No Holds Barred; René Clément; Robert Rossen; Montgomery Clift; Screen Acting; A Night In An English Music Hall; Steam in The 'Thirties'; Carné and Prévert; W. C. Fields; Screen Acting; Canals of Britain; Golden Age of The Cinema Organ; British Music Hall Command Performance; Best of British Films on Painting; Italy 1; The Short Film Scene (Part 1); By Gaslight; Screen Acting; Films for the Specialists; Italy 2; The Short Film Scene; Mason; Screen Acting; Experimental Scene; East and West; Young Film-Maker '67; Kings of Comedy No. 1 – Harry Langdon; Command Performance; Budapest Calling; A Programme of Hungarian Documentaries, Experimental and Cartoon Films; Screen Acting; Godard; Ten Days That Shook The World; Contemporary Soviet Cinema; More Than Human; 11th LFF; Galapagos Appeal.

1968. Adventures and Romance; Buster Keaton; Anatole de Grunwald; Richard Attenborough; Man With The Movie-Camera; Don Siegel – American Cinema; Buster Keaton – Part Two; Mamoulian; The New American Cinema; Human Rights; Danish Films; The '20s – How They Roared; World Cinema Review – Corner Stones; Anthony Asquith; The Royal College of Art; International Shorts Week; Rumanian Days; Forum Film and Environment; The John Player Lectures (start); Wilder; Alain Resnais – His Line and Circle; New Czechs; New Films from the Arts Council; The Outstanding Sponsored Films of 1968; Hitchcock; The Twelfth London Film Festival – 19th Nov. – 5th Dec. '68; Cukor; Donen; Foreman; Friday Night is Hitchcock Night; Pot Pourri; For the Specialist; LSFT; SFMC; Nicholas Ray Season.

1969. Spectaculars; World Cinema – Yugoslavia; Star Gazing; Charlton Heston – Then and Now; Tribute to Cinémathèque Française; Budd Boetticher Season; Columbia Story; Cornerstones; Cuban Film Week; Japanese Cinema; Silent Greats; Buster Keaton Festival; Revolution in the Cinema; Tribute to Hal Wallis; Samuel Fuller; London Film Festival Retrospective; 13th London Film Festival; Evolution of the Swashbuckler; Noël Coward; Friday Night is Hitchcock Night; Max Ophuls.

1970. NFT 1 Kurosawa; Bergman; Open Saturdays; Brazil; Germany/Film and Nazi Germany; Bulgaria – New Films; Animation; Lenin on Film; Israel – Emerging Cinema; USA – Western Tradition; France – Robert Bresson; Ingmar Bergman – Fridays; Poland – New Wave in the Making; T.V. Special Programmes; Ingmar Bergman Retrospective; Explorations of the Underground; Japanese Popular Cinema; All Night Shows; Dickens Centenary; Roger Corman Retrospective; Tribute to Walt Disney; History of the Cinema; International Underground Film Festival; British Cinema in the '70s; Best of Cinema City.

NFT 2 Premiere Loving Memory; A Tribute – Mervyn le Roy; Films From The National Film Archive; Jean Cocteau – Poet; Spotlight on Shorts; Lester James Peries – Neglected Artist; British Cinema – Seth Holt; For the Specialist; Silent Screen; Documentary Tradition.

APPENDIX D

THE JOHN PLAYER LECTURES (for the first two seasons)

George Axelrod
Sir Michael Balcon
Budd Boetticher
John Boorman
John and Roy Boulting
John Paddy Carstairs
Alberto Cavalcanti
Sir Noël Coward
Stanley Donen
Dr Christopher Evans
John Frankenheimer
Carl Foreman
Samuel Fuller
Lillian Gish
Graham Greene
Ray Harryhausen
Charlton Heston
Alfred Hitchcock
Professor I. C. Jarvie
Norman Jewison

Elia Kazan
Jesse Lasky, Jr.
Richard Lester
Jerry Lewis
James Mason
Sam Peckinpah
Abraham Polonsky
Vincent Price
Nicholas Ray
Satyajit Ray
Lee Remick
Robert Ryan
Delphine Seyrig
Rod Steiger
Jacques Tati
Professor A. J. P. Taylor
Jack Valenti
Billy Wilder
Michael Winner

Dirk Bogarde opened the third series in November 1970 and was followed in December by Peter Watkins

APPENDIX E

1st, 1957

The House of the Angel
(Torre Nilsson)
Duped Till Doomsday
(Jung-Alsen)
The Crimson Curtain (Astruc)
Porte des Lilas (Clair)
A Sunday Romance (Feher)
The Unvanquished (Ray)
Notti Bianchi (Visconti)
Notti de Cabiria (Fellini)
Throne of Blood (Kurosawa)
The Laplanders (Per Hoest)
Kanal (Wajda)
Seventh Seal (Bergman)
A Face in the Crowd (Kazan)
The Forty-First (Chukhrai)
Captain from Koepenick
(Käutner)

2nd, 1958

The Beach (Torre Nilsson)
The Wolf Trap (Weiss)
The Lovers (Malle)
Goha (Baratier)
A Matter of Dignity
(Cacoyannis)
At Midnight (Revesz)
The Smugglers (Máriássy)
Two Eyes-Twelve Hands
(Shantaram)
La Sfida (Rosi)
The Legend of Narayama
(Kinoshita)
Muhomatsu, The Rickshaw
Man (Inagaki)

Eva Wants to Sleep
(Chmielewski)
Last Day of Summer
(Konowicki/Laskowski)
Wild Strawberries (Bergman)
The Old Man of the Sea
(Sturges)
The House Where I Live
(Kulidzhanov/Segal)
Ilya Muromets (Ptushko)
Terminus Love (Tressler)
The Girl from Moorhof
(Ucicky)
H.8. (Tanhofer)

3rd 1959

Appassionata (Weiss)
Stars (Wolf)
Les Quatre Cents Coups
(Truffaut)
La Tête Contre Les Murs
(Franju)
Orfeu Negro (Camus)
The Sleepless Years
(Máriássy)
The House under the Rocks
(Makk)
The World of Apu (Ray)
The Usual 'Unknown Persons'
(Monicelli)
Equinox Flower (Ozu)
The Hidden Fortress
(Kurosawa)
Conflagration (Ichikawa)
Nazarin (Buñuel)
Farewells (Has)

The Train (Kawalerowicz)
So Close to Life (Bergman)
Power Among Men
Come Back Africa (Rogosin)
Crime and Punishment, USA
(Sanders)
The Savage Eye
(Maddow/Meyers/Strick)
At a High Price (Donskoi)
Somebody Else's Children
(Abouladze)
Train Without a Timetable
(Bulajic)

4th, 1960
Fin de Fiesta (Torre Nilsson)
Romeo, Juliet and Darkness
(Weiss)
Love's Confusion (Dudow)
La Règle du Jeu (complete
version) (Renoir)
Tirez sur le Pianiste (Truffaut)
Les Jeux de l'Amour
(de Broca)
Moderato Cantabile (Brook)
Les Bonnes Femmes (Chabrol)
Our Last Spring (Cacoyannis)
For Whom the Lark Sings
(Ranódy)
Be Good Forever (Ranódy)
Jalsaghar (Ray)
Notte Brava (Bolognini)
L'Avventura (Antonioni)
Rocco and his Brothers
(Visconti)
Bad Boys (Hani)
The Young One (Buñuel)
Bad Luck (Munk)
Los Golfos (Saura)
El Cochecito (Ferreri)
Virgin Spring (Bergman)
Studs Lonigan (Lerner)
Flight (Bispo)
The Lady with the Little Dog
(Heifetz)

Ballad of a Soldier
(Chukhrai)
White Nights (Pyriev)
The Ninth Circle (Stiglic)

5th, 1961
Summer Skin (Torre Nilsson)
The Hand in the Trap
(Torre Nilsson)
Une Aussi Longue Absence
(Colpi)
Une Femme est une Femme
(Godard)
Léon Morin, Priest (Melville)
Tire au Flanc (de Givray)
Lola (Demy)
Antigone (Tzavellas)
Wedding Day (Sen)
Description of a Struggle
(Marker)
Accattone (Pasolini)
L'Assassino (Petri)
Il Posto (Olmi)
The Bad Sleep Well
(Kurosawa)
Fires on the Plain (Ichikawa)
The Island (Shindo)
The Devil's Eye (Bergman)
The Exiles (Mockenzie)
Too Late Blues (Cassavetes)
Clear Sky (Chukhrai)
Kolka My Friend
(Saltikov/Mitta)
Story of the Turbulent Years
(Sointseva)
Life of Adolf Hitler (Rotha)
Miracles of Malachias
(Wicki)

6th, 1962
The Sad Young Men (Kuhn)
Baron Munchausen (Zeman)
Homage at Siesta Time
(Torre Nilsson)
Darling (Kurkvaara)

N

A Heart As Big As That
(Reichenbach)
Vivre sa Vie (Godard)
The Olive Trees of Justice
(Blue)
The Trial of Joan of Arc
(Bresson)
The Vanishing Corporal
(Renoir)
The Loneliness of the Long
Distance Runner
(Richardson)
Elektra (Zarpas)
The Grim Reaper (Bertolucci)
Il Mare (Patroni Griffi)
The New Angels (Gregoretti)
Devi (Ray)
Early Autumn (Ozu)
Sanjuro (Kurosawa)
The Exterminating Angel
(Buñuel)
Knife in the Water (Polanski)
Placido (Berlanga)
Football (Drew)
War Hunt (Sanders)
The Bread of Our Early Years
(Veseley)
The Siberian Lady Macbeth
(Wajda)

7th, 1963

Paula Cautiva (Ayala)
The Roofgarden
(Torre Nilsson)
Barravento (Rocha)
The Golden Fern (Weiss)
The Russian Miracle
(The Thorndikes)
La Belle Vie (Enrico)
Au Coeur de la Vie (Enrico)
Le Joli Mai (Marker)
En Compagnie de Max Linder
(Linder)
Le Feu Follet (Malle)
L'Aîné des Ferchaux (Melville)

Les Carabiniers (Godard)
Dragées au Poivre (Baratier)
Muriel (Resnais)
The Trial (Welles)
Ouranos (Kanelopoulos)
Love in the Suburbs (Fejer)
I Basilischi (Wertmüller)
The Engagement (Olmi)
Hands over the City (Rosi)
Il Demonio (Rondi)
Rogopag (Rossellini/Godard/
Pasolini/Gregoretti)
An Autumn Afternoon (Ozu)
How To Be Loved (Has)
Passenger (Munk)
The Executioner (Berlanga)
A Sunday in September
(Donner)
The Balcony (Strick)
The Chair (Drew)
Hallelujah the Hills (Mekas)
Harold Lloyd's Funny Side of
Life
Wild Dog Dingo (Karasik)

8th, 1964

The Inheritance (Alventosa)
Nobody Waved Goodbye
(Owen)
Joseph Kilian
(Schmidt/Juráček)
Peter and Pavla (Forman)
La Vie à L'Envers (Jessua)
La Baie des Anges (Demy)
Bande à Part (Godard)
Les Parapluies de Cherbourg
(Demy)
Diary of a Chambermaid
(Buñuel)
Cyrano et d'Artagnan (Gance)
It Happened Here
(Brownlow/Mollo)
King and Country (Losey)
The Logic Game (Saville)
Current (Gaàl)

Mahanagar (Ray)
Before the Revolution
  (Bertolucci)
The Novice (Paolinelli)
The Gospel According to
  Matthew (Pasolini)
She and He (Hani)
Woman of the Dream
  (Teshigahara)
Alone on the Pacific
  (Ichikawa)
Personal Characteristics
  (Skolimowski)
To Love (Donner)
Raven's End (Widerberg)
Across the River (Sharff)
The Brig (Mekas)
Nothing But A Man Roemer)
Point of Order (de Antonio)

9th, 1965
  Caressed (Kent)
  A Blonde in Love (Forman)
  Gertrud (Dreyer)
  The Lion Hunt (Rouch)
  Le Mystère Koumiko (Marker)
  Six in Paris (Rouch/Rohmer/
    Godard/Chabrol, etc.)
  Thomas L'Imposteur (Franju)
  Alphaville (Godard)
  L'Or du Duc (Baratier)
  Pierrot le Fou (Godard)
  Ascent (Sinha)
  Kapurush-O-Mahapurush
    (Ray)
  Shakespeare-Wallah (Ivory)
  Fists in the Pocket
    (Bellocchio)
  The Moment of Truth (Rosi)
  Jose Torres (Teshigahara)
  Red Beard (Kurosawa)
  Manuscript Found in Saragossa
    (Has)
  Walkover (Skolimowski)
  Dear John (Lindgren)

Harvey Middleman, Fireman
  (Pintoff)
Lady in a Cage (Grauman)
Mickey One (Penn)
The Enchanted Desna
  (Solntseva)
Nicht Versöhnt (Straub)
Seven Chances (Keaton)

10th, 1966
  Barrier (Skolimowski)
  Yesterday Girl (Kluge)
  The Battle of Algiers
    (Pontecorvo)
  Winter Kept Us Warm (Secter)
  Bwana Toshi (Hani)
  The Shameless Old Lady
    (Allio)
  The Hunt (Saura)
  The Eavesdropper
    (Torre Nilsson)
  Echoes of Silence (Goldman)
  Every Young Man (Juracek)
  The Face of Another
    (Teshigahara)
  Intimate Lighting (Passer)
  Lenin in Poland (Yutkevich)
  The Long March (Astruc)
  Made in U.S.A. (Godard)
  The Man Who Had His Hair
    Cut Short (Delvaux)
  To Die in Madrid (Rossif)
  Father Christmas Has Blue Eyes
    (Eustache)
  The Rise of Louis XIV
    (Rossellini)
  The Private Right (Papas)
  Seven Women (Ford)
  If I Had Four Dromedaries
    (Marker)
  Shadows of Our Forgotten
    Ancestors (Paradzhanov)
  The Hawks and the Sparrows
    (Pasolini)
  Almost a Man (De Seta)

11th, 1967

Father (Szabo)
Bezhin Meadow
  (after Eisenstein)
La Chinoise (Godard)
La Collectionneuse (Rohmer)
Les Creatures (Varda)
Le Départ (Skolimowski)
Deux ou Trois Choses que je
  sais d'elle (Godard)
Elvira Madigan (Widerberg)
Dreamers (Stenbaek)
Funnyman (Korty)
Rebellion (Kobayashi)
Young Torless (Schlöndorff)
Switchboard Operator
  (Makavejev)
Far from Vietnam (Resnais,
  Klein, Ivens, Varda, Le-
  louch, Godard)
Mouchette (Bresson)
Martyrs of Love (Nemec)
Portrait of Jason (Clarke)
Hugs and Kisses (Cornell)
Rondo (Berkovic)
Daisies (Chytilova)
Heart of a Mother (Donskoi)
Simon of the Desert (Buñuel)
Tonite Let's All Make Love in
  London and The Benefit of
  the Doubt (Whitehead)
The Feverish Years (Lazic)
Trans-Europ Express
  (Robbe-Grillet)
L'Une et l'Autre (Allio)
A Mother's Devotion
  (Donskoi)

12th, 1968

Adelaide (Simon)
The Artistes at the Top of the
  Big Top: Disorientated
  (Kluge)
Stolen Kisses (Truffaut)
Les Biches (Chabrol)

The Chronicle of Anna Magda-
  lena Bach (Straub)
They Call Us Misfits
  (Lindqvist/Jarl)
The Immortal Story (Welles)
The Fireman's Ball (Forman)
Don't Look Back (Pennebaker)
L'Enfance Nue (Pialat)
Kaya (Mimica)
Signs of Life (Herzog)
Hugo and Josefin (Grede)
If . . . (Anderson)
Black on White (Jörn Donner)
Who Saw Him Die? (Troell)
Memories of Underdevelopment
  (Alea)
Monsieur Hawarden (Kümel)
Capricious Summer (Menzel)
The Secret Life of an American
  Wife (Axelrod)
One Plus One (Godard)
Shame (Bergman)
The Delinquent (Schaaf)
Tropics (Amico)
Everything for Sale (Wajda)

13th, 1969

One Fine Day (Olmi)
Destroy, She Says (Duras)
The Event (Mimica)
Duet for Cannibals (Sontag)
A Nest of Gentlefolk
  (Mikhalkov-Konchalovsky)
Events (Llewellyn)
A Gentle Creature (Bresson)
The Confrontation (Jancso)
Horoscope (Draskovic)
Je t'aime, je t'aime (Resnais)
Kes (Loach)
Death by Hanging (Oshima)
Lions Love (Varda)
Mandabi (Sembene)
My Night with Maud
  (Rohmer)
Pierre et Paul (Allio)

Pigsty (Pasolini)
Prologue (Spry)
Le Samouri (Melville)
Double Suicide (Shinoda)
Boy (Oshĭma)
Un Soir – Un Train
 (Delvaux)
Sweet Hunters (Guerra)
The Lady from Constantinople
 (Elek)
La Trêve (Guillemot)
The Deserter and the Nomads
 (Jakubisko)
The Joke (Jires)

14th, 1970
 Days and Nights in the Forest
  (Satyajit Ray)
 Even Dwarfs Started Small
  (Herzog)
 Bartleby (Friedmann)
 Le Boucher (Chabrol)
 The Cannibals (Cavani)
 The Conformist (Bertolucci)
 Deep End (Skolimowski)
 Dodeska-Den (Kurosawa)

L'Enfant Sauvage (Truffaut)
Eros+ Massacre (Yoshida)
The Färö Document (Bergman)
La Faute de l'Abbé Mouret
 (Franju)
Hoa-Binh (Coutard)
Landscape after Battle (Wajda)
The Handcuffs (Papić)
The Falcons (Gaál)
The Night of the Counting of
 the Years (Abdelsalam)
Petit à Petit (Rouch)
Quiet Days in Clichy
 (Thorsen)
The Scavengers (Olmi)
Ramparts of Clay (Bertuccelli)
Master of the Land (Thiago)
The Spider's Strategy
 (Bertolucci)
Tristana (Buñuel)
Valerie and the Week of
 Wonders (Jires)
The Crows (Kozomara and
 Mihic)
Wanda (Loden)
The Garden of Delight (Saura)

Index